THE COMPLETE POEMS

EDWIN DENBY

THE COMPLETE POEMS

Edited and with an introduction by Ron Padgett
and with essays by Frank O'Hara
and Lincoln Kirstein

Photographs by Rudy Burckhardt

RANDOM HOUSE NEW YORK

Library of Congress Cataloging-in-Publication Data

Denby, Edwin, 1903–
The complete poems.
I. Padgett, Ron. II. Title.
PS3507.E54339A17 1986   811'.54   85-18384
ISBN 0-394-54404-8
ISBN 0-394-74344-X (pbk.)

24689753

First Paperback Edition

ACKNOWLEDGMENTS

I am very grateful to the following people for help in the preparation of this book. Rudy Burckhardt and Yvonne Jacquette, executors of the estate of Edwin Denby, gave me complete cooperation and freedom in working with Edwin's papers. Rudy also provided the photographs that head each section in this volume, as well as much of the information in its introduction. Robert Cornfield was a friend of Edwin's who became one of his editors and then also his agent. I appreciate his helping see this book through. Bill MacKay was extraordinarily helpful in sorting Edwin's papers, deciphering his script, and alerting me to new material. George Schneeman, Kenward Elmslie, Patricia Padgett, and Bill Berkson made many valuable suggestions for the introduction. Lincoln Kirstein allowed me to use a revised version of his article that originally appeared in the *New York Review of Books*, and Maureen O'Hara granted permission to reprint Frank O'Hara's essay on Edwin's poetry. I am also grateful to my colleagues at Full Court Press, Joan Simon and Anne Waldman, for help with Edwin's *Collected Poems* and for granting permission to reprint it in its entirety. Alice Notley knows Edwin's poems as well as she does her own: I thank her for her vigilant proofreading. I also thank Walter E. DeMelle, Jr., of the Hotchkiss School and Francis Mason of the Morgan Library for helping obtain copies of Edwin's early poems, and Amy Fague of the Hotchkiss Alumni Society and Lucy Wu of Harvard for providing documents relating to Edwin's academic life. Jonathan Galassi at Random House welcomed *The Complete Poems* with the cordiality that all of Edwin's friends were hoping for.

CONTENTS

City Seasons and **Snoring in New York**

Later Sonnets

Other Poems

INTRODUCTION

It is unusual for a poet's first collection from a major publisher to be a *Complete Poems*. In Edwin Denby's case, however, it is understandable. Edwin never "built his career" as poet. He never did anything to make his poetry known to a wide audience. In fact, by the 1960s he had become skittish about having his poetry published at all.

His first book, *In Public, In Private* (1948), had shown signs of this nervousness. The first edition, published by Decker Press in Prairie City, Illinois, was followed by a second edition only a few months later, not because the first had sold out but because Edwin (in New York and preparing to go to Europe) saw the need for alterations. He revised certain lines, dropped one poem, and corrected typographical errors. There must have been a certain amount of torment in seeing a whole new group of mistakes in the second edition. Edwin, his friends, and one of his brothers had underwritten the cost of both editions.

They also subsidized the second collection of poems, *Mediterranean Cities* (1956). This time, perhaps in reaction to the misprints in *In Public, In Private*, Edwin chose an outstanding printer, the Stamperia Valdonega in Verona, Italy. The production was handled by mail, with manuscripts, photographs, and proofs shuttling back and forth between Verona and New York. I suspect Edwin intentionally maintained his geographical distance from the production of this book, as he had with *In Public, In Private*.

Despite their literary excellence, these books did not reach a large audience. Neither Decker Press nor George Wittenborn, Inc. (credited on the title page of *Mediterranean Cities* as its publisher) had an advertising, sales, or distribution system for poetry. And Edwin's modesty, perhaps a result of his being well brought up, disallowed his behaving as though the public should admire him. His friends knew that an easy way to make him nervous was to praise him, especially for the wrong reasons: he would quickly change the subject or glance nervously toward the nearest exit. But people did admire him, a small, select audience of friends and those who were to become friends; poets such as Frank O'Hara and James Schuyler; painters such as Willem and Elaine de Kooning, Alex Katz, and Neil Welliver; composers such as Virgil Thomson and Aaron Copland; dancers and choreographers such as Merce Cunningham, Tanaquil LeClerc, and Paul Taylor; and his close friend Rudy Burckhardt, whose photographs were an added delight in Edwin's books.

In the early 1960s a new wave of admirers began to arrive. These young poets, painters, and dancers ferreted out rare copies of Edwin's books and, in their youthful ardor, tended to view him as a sort of living legend. Chief among these was Ted Berrigan, the poet and editor. When Ted admired the work of someone who was, in his opinion, neglected, he set about correcting the situation. He wrote and spoke about Edwin's work with such conviction and persuasiveness that one was left with no choice but to read Edwin's poetry and begin to see for oneself.* Ted brought the same magnanimous intensity to the special Edwin Denby issue of his magazine *C* (1963), the first Denby collection of poems published by someone other than the author. I was with Ted the August night he swooped down on Edwin and declared that he was going to do the issue and that it would appear in a few weeks, so Edwin should now please immediately give him some new, unpublished poems to go with the older ones. Edwin, disarmed by this irrepressible Irishman, could hardly refuse what apparently was a *fait accompli*. The issue did in fact appear soon after, each copy bearing original silk-screened front and back covers by Andy Warhol, with an arresting image of Edwin being kissed by a young man. Edwin had little say in all this.

This was equally true of his next collection, *Snoring in New York* (1974), co-published by Anne Waldman of Angel Hair and Larry Fagin of Adventures in Poetry. Comprised mostly of Edwin's later sonnets, this booklet served as an advance glimpse into another volume, already in preparation, his *Collected Poems*.

The *Collected Poems* was published in 1975 by Full Court Press (Anne Waldman, Joan Simon, and me). We knew we couldn't wait for Edwin's permission to print the book: he would hesitate forever. So we simply told him we were starting a publishing company and that the first book would consist of his poems. We didn't elicit the kind of conversation that would give him a chance to delay or refuse. Anytime he did mutter something about how no one would want to read his poetry because it was "just old stuff and not good enough," it was we who changed the subject and glanced toward the exit.

Right up to the publication of the *Collected Poems*, Edwin feared it would become overblown. He adamantly refused to allow the book to be called *The Complete Poems*, even though he had pretty much stopped writing poetry by then. That title sounded too pompous, too "uptown" for him (and perhaps too final). Also, he would not let us publish five of his later sonnets because he was "still working on them."

Without our knowing it, he paid someone else to correct the proofs. Was he unable to bear what he felt to be the inadequacies of his poetry,

---

* Ted "converted" me. I had first read Edwin's poetry in *Locus Solus* (No. 1, 1961), but I don't remember when I first met him in the following few years. My most vivid early memory of him is of running into him at a double-feature of Hammer horror films at the New Yorker Theater in late 1963—he was doing "research" for his mad scientist role in Burckhardt's film *Lurk*—and his coming back to my apartment for coffee and conversation. He became only mildly discombobulated when I asked him to autograph my copy of *In Public, In Private*.

or did the poetry have such evocative power for him that it was too painful to reread? Or both?

The *Collected Poems* received highly favorable notices. Bill Zavatsky wrote: "Denby's *Collected Poems* is an important Baedecker by a sharp-eyed man who has noted down, with love, what most of us rush right past. Delightful work."[1] Jonathan Galassi praised it as "a living, breathing, unusually valuable book by a poet who should be better known."[2] Hayden Carruth noted that Edwin had "been around for years actually, but fugitive, very fugitive" and that Edwin's work has "the enduring voice of poetry, the essential voice which carries on in spite of everything that fashion and literary politics can do to silence it."[3] Michael Lally echoed these sentiments: "It's obvious from [Denby's] work that many poets have been influenced by it, but where are the critics who mention it, or the anthologies that include it? This is not the incidental poetry of an eminent dance critic, or the work of an underground cult figure, but the work of a unique and major voice in contemporary poetry."[4] The consensus was one of bewilderment that this work had not been available before and of gratitude that now it was.

Edwin's reaction to all this was typically ambivalent. Rudy Burckhardt told me that Edwin claimed he didn't like all the attention but that deep down he was pleased by it. It was not the embittered pleasure of someone "recognized" too late, nor the preening pleasure of the vain. It was the pleasure of an old gentleman who had realized that his work was well loved.

The *Complete Poems* includes all the poems in the 1975 *Collected Poems*, some of which had appeared with typographical errors, others which Edwin revised slightly. (In December of 1982 he gave me a list of such corrections and revisions, which stand as the final ones.) To these works I have added a few untitled poems that have never appeared in book form: " 'It takes all kinds,' the hackie's saw"; "In a hotelroom a madman"; "At first sight, not Pollock, Kline scared"; "The newspaper lies slid, tracked up"; "In tooth and claw red, not nature"; and two versions of "Old age, lookit, it's stupid, a big fart." Edwin would probably have objected to their inclusion. It was only after his death, in looking through his manuscripts and notebooks, that I realized how hard he had worked on his later poems, revising them over and over, scratching out lines and then restoring them, only to scratch them out again. He worked several sonnets so hard that they slimmed down to only thirteen lines.

This *Complete Poems* does not include, of course, every poem Edwin wrote and saved. I have excluded poems written in adolescence, poems

[1] *New York Times Book Review*, October 17, 1976.
[2] *Poetry*, December 1976.
[3] *Bookletter*, March 15, 1976.
[4] *Washington Post Book World*, February 8, 1976.

in a fragmentary state, and poems he had abandoned but not discarded. Not that there are many such pieces. In fact, given that he occupied the same loft for almost half a century, it is surprising how few papers he did keep. His austerity was pervasive. He was anything but his own archivist; he never dated his manuscripts, he never made marginal notes other than "out," "reject," or "keep," and he never kept his papers in any particular order. Finally, he made no special attempt to preserve them; as of this writing, the early manuscript versions of the poems in *In Public, In Private* and most of those in *Mediterranean Cities* remain lost.

Although Edwin was ambivalent about seeing his poetry in print and never played any standard role of "the poet," it is clear, from works such as the following undated, unrevised, and unpublished piece, that he did see himself as part of a literary tradition, a "print of voices" from Walt Whitman to himself to Frank O'Hara:

> Moved by a three A.M. breeze, an empty paper bag scrapes on the floor at the back of the loft—a thief sound—a wind from building to building bayward where the tide flows—exposed alone to electric light I sit reading poems of Frank O'Hara's—the print of voices dead Walt heard nervously in barroom and bedroom and I did and Frank does—the summer, the winter, a voice's fleshly furtive circling pitch among voices closeby, echoing Manhattan island closeby and far like Venice or Rotterdam or Leningrad or Foochow to be obliterated friends asleep on salt water sites or by electric light reading recent poems nearly single in the heat at night hearing the police or song behind a wall, a recent century of multiple acquainted voices, closeby, far off, silly, unobliterated, mine too, yours too.

Edwin Orr Denby was born on February 4, 1903, in Tientsin, China. His father, Charles Denby, Jr., the American Consul in Tientsin and later a businessman, had met his mother, Martha Orr, in Peking, where her family had stopped on a trip around the world. Martha Orr's father was a businessman too, and both the Denby and the Orr families were from Evansville, Indiana. Edwin's grandfather, Charles Denby, Sr., had served as minister to China in the mid-1880s, and he was illustrious enough to have the Charles Denby cigar named after him. Edwin was named after his paternal uncle, who was Secretary of the Navy under Harding and who had the honor of throwing out the first ball in Yankee Stadium. In 1924, however, charged with neglect of duty in the Teapot Dome scandal, he resigned, apparently a scapegoat.

After stays in Washington, D.C., and Hannover, Germany, the Denbys returned to China. One of Edwin's early memories was "at age four, that was in Shanghai . . . I remember the house, and pagoda, that marvelous thing with the great big tower in the back yard was overturned outside the wall of our garden, and it was so amazing to see it lying there on the ground."[5] The image of the pagoda—the exotic edifice that is both tower and temple, with curled-up eaves on its roofs that diminish as they gracefully rise—sideways on the ground can be applied in some respects to Edwin and his work. From birth—an American born in China—he was out of place. Dislocation, though, brought surprise and pleasure, as well as the isolation of being different. His dislocation in China was doubled: he was not only removed from America, but, like his two older brothers and most of the other children of diplomats and foreign businessmen, he was restricted to the European community, removed from the Chinese.

Unlike the pagoda, however, Edwin was throughout his life mobile and fascinated by mobility, the mobility of travel, of dancers, of his cats, of strolling through the streets, and of thought.

When his family left Shanghai (in 1908, after Edwin's tonsils were removed) they settled in Vienna, where his father had another diplomatic appointment. Edwin received his early schooling in Vienna, where he learned German and saw his first ballet, *Die Puppenfee (The Fairy Doll)*, which made a powerful impression on him. He was having dinner with his family on vacation at one of the grand hotels at the Lido when the outbreak of World War I was announced. Again Edwin was to find himself in an incongruous situation: eventually his family had to leave Austria, "the enemy country we had all liked so much."[6]

Returning for the first time to live for an extended period in the country of his nationality, he briefly attended private school in Detroit, where his father took a position as vice president of the Hupp Motor Company. In 1916, Edwin was sent to Hotchkiss, the Connecticut preparatory school. He had started writing poetry around the age of twelve, and by fourteen showed a precocious talent for the sonnet, as shown in his second published poem:

Sonnet

Then, in the dewy even-tide of years,
We'll sit together, while the feline night
Steals silently without, and the faint light
Of low-burned candles trembles as wind nears;
We'll sit together on the rude-carved bench
I made for you when first our eyes had met.—
Ah! What a moment!—Ne'er shall I forget
Those eyes,—whose light of trust no years can quench.

[5] In an interview with Mark Hillringhouse, *Mag City* No. 14, 1983.
[6] Quoted in *The Party's Over Now* by John Gruen (New York: Viking, 1972), p. 162.

Then will the fiery passions of the May
Of Life be tempered by maturer age;
Then eyes will dim and thin the golden tress,
And cheeks grow pale—past long their triumph day.
And though not far the threatening death-storms rage,
Yet Love lives in the bare boughs none the less![7]

At Hotchkiss he wrote sonnets influenced by Milton, Wordsworth, and Shelley. He also wrote the class poem. In his senior year he was voted "The Biggest Grind" by his classmates, "those other fellows whom I didn't get along with."[8] Edwin had an outstanding scholastic record; his scores on the college entrance examinations were the highest in the country. In 1919 he graduated, winning the Phi Beta Kappa trophy and the Greek and English prizes. Hotchkiss was a feeder school for Yale; Edwin, not yet seventeen, went to Harvard.

His freshman year was academically outstanding, but in December 1920, in the middle of his sophomore year, he abruptly left school and took a steamer to England with classmate Frank Safford. They expected to go there and make their fortunes, but they soon returned, penniless, and this slender, sensitive, well-traveled young poet took a job for five months on a New Hampshire farm.

Seeing no other option, he went back to Harvard in 1921 for another year, but was not happy there, cutting classes, reading poetry, drinking, dreaming, and talking with a few good friends, feeling "wanderlust," and hoping to write some day "with fire."[9]

Edwin did not return to Harvard for his junior year. Instead he and Safford quit school again and moved (with Safford's wife) to New York City "to study and write," neither of which they did. Typically, Edwin landed an unsuitable job (with the New York Telephone Company), which he quit after five months because, although he understood perfectly the abstract wiring diagrams, he was bewildered by masses of real wires. His parents must have been apprehensive about him, but they gave him some money, and with it he went in 1923 to Vienna, partly because Safford was going to study medicine there.

To keep his parents happy, Edwin enrolled in a few courses at the University of Vienna. On the train, returning to Vienna after a vacation, he fell into conversation with a young woman who invited him to see the Hellerau-Laxenburg School, where she was studying dance. Urged on by friends, and to keep his promise to her, he visited the school. Soon afterward he enrolled and took his first dance lessons. Again, he found himself out of place: he was one of the few male students.

[7] *The Hotchkiss Literary Monthly*, May 1917.
[8] Hillringhouse.
[9] From an unpublished diary.

xvi

There were, however, more fundamental problems than this. He had doubtless dismayed his parents by dropping out of college and not getting ahead. He seemed to have no marketable skills, no place in society. And by now he, who had been dismayed by the snickering remarks of homophobic college classmates, must have recognized that he was having trouble coming to terms with his sexuality. During this period in Vienna he experienced depression and considered suicide, but "never had the nerve."[10] One day he knocked on Dr. Freud's door and was told that the doctor was indisposed but that Dr. Paul Federn, a colleague, could be consulted. Edwin underwent analysis with Dr. Federn for several years, and later met Freud through him. Federn's other patients included (though not at the same time) Rilke, Wilhelm Reich, and Hermann Broch.

After three years (1925–1928) at the Hellerau-Laxenburg School, Edwin received a diploma in gymnastics, which led to his specializing in *Grotesktanz* ("eccentric dancing"), a form of modern dance. After a brief period as a member of the dancing chorus of the State Theater of Darmstadt, he and his partner Claire Eckstein formed a small dance company. The group toured Germany (1928–1933), appearing at the Berlin Wintergarten and receiving favorable reviews in German dance magazines that singled out his work for praise. Photographs of Edwin performing *Grotesktanz* reflect the image of the pagoda on its side: he is usually shown in surprising positions.

Two of his poems appeared in *Poetry* in 1926, apparently the first publication of his poetry in a national literary magazine. How this occurred remains unknown.

In 1927 his oldest brother, Charles, sent him round-trip fare so he could return to America for both brothers' weddings (which turned out to be prestigious affairs, with prominent guests attending James's wedding in Philadelphia and a week later President and Mrs. Coolidge attending Charles's in Washington, D.C.). Knowing that Edwin would have little interest in these social events, Charles assured him that he could spend the travel money any way he liked. So Edwin, the odd man out in his family, took a trip to Russia, staying for six weeks in Moscow. There, on a pass personally issued by Anatoly Lunacharsky—the writer, revolutionary, and powerful Commissar of Education in charge of Theaters—he saw many productions (including one of Meyerhold's) and the Bolshoi Ballet.

In 1929, with his passport still listing his occupation as "student," he returned to the State Theater of Darmstadt and spent a year as dancer, choreographer, and libretto adapter. His colleagues there included Wilhelm Reinking and Rudolf Bing. Edwin's German libretto *Die Neue Galathea*, an adaptation of Franz von Suppe's operetta *Die Schoene Galathea*, was performed in 1929 and published by B. Schott's Sons, Mainz.

[10] Hillringhouse.

xvii

He tried, without success, to convince his colleagues to produce Gertrude Stein and Virgil Thomson's *Four Saints in Three Acts*, still unperformed at that time. In the late 1920s in Germany, Edwin met Aaron Copland, Bertolt Brecht, Kurt Weill, and Lotte Lenya. Much of Edwin's own output during this period—adaptations, stories, essays, perhaps poems and theater pieces—was written in German.

In Collioure, France, in 1930, Edwin met Virgil Thomson, who was to remain a lifelong friend. Considering Edwin's circle of acquaintances and his numerous if brief trips to Paris, it is odd that he never met Gertrude Stein, whose work had a noticeable influence on his poetry.

Germany grew increasingly dangerous, and because Edwin's satirical dances were considered politically suspect he left in 1933. In Paris later that same year a performance of Balanchine's work—which he had first seen in 1930—struck him as "the most wonderful thing I had seen in my life," especially *Mozartiana*.[11] It was at this point that Edwin began to take a serious interest in ballet. In the 1940s he championed Balanchine in New York, and his admiration never wavered.

Edwin joined his family in Majorca, where he wrote the first draft of his only novel, *Scream in a Cave* (also called *Mrs. W's Last Sandwich*).

In 1934, in need of a new passport photo, he met the photographer-medical student Rudy Burckhardt in Basel. Having spent the past several years moving around Europe, Edwin returned to New York in 1935, soon followed by Burckhardt, and together they rented the cold-water, heatless, fifth-floor walk-up loft at 145 West 21 Street that he was to occupy for the rest of his life. Though heat and hot water were later added, the loft always retained its austerity.

He soon became friends with his neighbor Willem (and soon thereafter Elaine) de Kooning. It was fortuitous and wonderful that they happened to live in the building just next door. Edwin and Burckhardt sat for de Kooning and were among the first to buy his work; that is, from time to time they gave him money when he needed it and from time to time he gave them a picture.

For the next ten years Edwin produced a great deal, mostly in New York, a city flooded with refugee artists and intellectuals. He wrote the poems published in 1948 as *In Public, In Private*. He also wrote adaptations and librettos: *Horse Eats Hat* with Orson Welles, a W.P.A. adaptation of Labiche and Michel's *Le Chapeau de paille d'Italie*, with incidental music by Paul Bowles orchestrated by Virgil Thomson (premiere in 1936, with Edwin playing the rear legs of the horse, designed by puppeteer Bil Baird); *The Second Hurricane*, an opera libretto with music by Aaron Copland (premiere in 1937); *The Sonntag Gang*, an opera libretto (completed in 1940); a ballet libretto, *The Death and Some Notes on the Life of*

[11]Interview with John Howell, *Performance Arts Journal #11*, Vol. 4, Nos. 1–2, n.d.

Joe Bascom (completed in 1941); and *Miltie Is a Hackie*, an opera libretto (completed in 1942). With Rita Matthias he translated Bruckner's play *The Criminals* (premiere in 1941). He also did the choreography (for the Boston premiere only) of the Maxwell Anderson–Kurt Weill musical, *Knickerbocker Holiday* (1938) and appeared for the first of many times in films of Burckhardt's.

His librettos and adaptations are mostly about America, with high school students, cowboys, blacks, a jockey, a cab driver, and so on, using language that is often downright "down home." It is as though he were studying the same faces as those in the photographs of his friend Walker Evans. Edwin's "common man" subject matter, however, never quite took on the proletariat slant typical of the 1930s, for although he was antifascist (and even anticapitalist), he played no active part in politics. In writing about ordinary Americans, he was trying to see what it felt like to be one. He was also clarifying his language, making it simpler and sleeker. Like Gertrude Stein and William Carlos Williams, two other somewhat dislocated Americans, he worked with a simple vocabulary to express complex feelings. It should be added that Edwin took great pleasure in being in New York, among people he didn't particularly understand.

At Aaron Copland's suggestion he wrote articles on the dance (his first was "Noces," 1936) and that same year—again through Copland—began a regular dance review column ("With the Dancers") for Minna Lederman's *Modern Music*, partly, he claimed, as a way of getting free tickets. He credited Lederman with having taught him how to rein in his tendency toward poetic digression and to express himself more clearly in essay form.

In 1937 he passed through Puerto Rico and the Dominican Republic on his way to Haiti with Burckhardt, then went to stay in Mexico with Copland to work on *The Second Hurricane*.

After the bombing of Pearl Harbor, he tried to enlist in the Army, but was refused, apparently because of his age (nearly thirty-nine). At Virgil Thomson's invitation he worked as guest dance critic for the New York *Herald Tribune* from 1942 until 1945 (when the regular critic, Walter Terry, returned from war). Edwin's working pattern as a critic underwent a sudden change: the same critic who had labored painfully over every word in his *Modern Music* pieces could now finish a review for the morning edition a few hours after leaving an evening performance. The drain on his energy was telling, though, and he relinquished the job with as much relief as regret.

The appearance of his first book of poems, *In Public, In Private*, was delayed by the war until 1948. The scant critical response ranged from lukewarm to mixed to thoroughly negative. The most favorable notice, by Hubert Creekmore, praised Edwin's "flair for finishing off his poems with a meaningful couplet, for combining the traditional epigram with the lyric, and for ironic effects," for the "many truly astonishing images," and for their forming "a witty or revealing series of comments," but noted that the work needed more "focus and unification and smoothness," that it was "diffused in impact because subjectively organized."[12] British critic Nicolas Moore felt that although the poems' language and imagery were "striking," "Mr. Denby lacks control."[13] The two other American reviews were both by Dudley Fitts. In the *Kenyon Review*[14] he allowed that four of the poems were worthy of book publication, but in the *Partisan Review* he blasted the author for having "neither taste, nor ear, nor control," with little in the book other than "mishandled metres, a yammering diction, and a brash inconsequence of intent."[15] Given the prevailing poetic climate in the late 1940s, it is not hard to see how these reviewers mistook the compressed, quirky, big-city stop-and-go rhythms for lack of control. These rhythms have little to do with, say, the artful "sprung" rhythm of Gerard Manley Hopkins' poetry or even the fragmented measures of Pound's *Cantos*. The work in *In Public, In Private* is further complicated by its coupling of idiomatic language and traditional form, making Edwin a kind of unpredictable Shakespeare-Wordsworth of the streets. It was hard to categorize—and thereby understand—his poetry.

If these are hard poems to read, they are not hard in the usual ways: they are not recondite, they are not high-toned, they do not make literary allusions, they do not use "poetic" language. They are not even aggressively modernist or "experimental" (although in their own subtle way they are quite radical). Their difficulties lie elsewhere, particularly in their shifting tones.

Take, for instance, the first four lines of the first poem, "The Climate":

> I myself like the climate of New York
> I see it in the air up between the street
> You use a worn-down cafeteria fork
> But the climate you don't use stays fresh and neat

The first line seems like a simple enough beginning. But what's this word "myself" doing there? Its presence suggests that the first line is not the start of a train of thought, but rather the continuation of an anterior clause such as "Some people don't care for the weather here, but. . . ." The first line, then, has a little accent or inflection in the reflexive pronoun that shifts the tone of what would otherwise be an ordinary opening. The first line ends with no punctuation other than blank space, which

[12] *New York Times Book Review*, August 15, 1948.
[13] *Poetry Quarterly* (London), Vol. 10, No. 3, Autumn 1948.
[14] Vol. 11, No. 1, Winter 1949.
[15] Vol. 16, No. 4, April 1949.

in Edwin's poetry usually indicates a pause; he doesn't use punctuation marks unless they're necessary for clarity or emphasis.

Like the first line, the second uses simple language with a shift in it, but this time the shift is semantic. Oddly, the speaker *sees the climate*, which suggests a wider range of perception than does, say, seeing a cloud. What is more arresting, though, is that he uses the phrase "up between the street." "Street," in this context, assumes its more inclusive meaning of pavement, curbs, sidewalks, and buildings. What is understood here is "up between the *sides* of the street," because obviously nothing can be between one thing.

Line three contains another tonal shift. What appears on first reading to be a flat statement is in fact inflected: there is emphasis on "use" (in the sense of "use up"): "You *use* a worn-down cafeteria fork," in opposition to line four, "But the climate you don't use stays fresh and neat." The unexpectedly domestic vocabulary ("fresh and neat") to describe something as intangible and all-encompassing as climate is another example of the delicate but significant moves in the poem.

These nimble shifts—a form of wit characteristic of Edwin's poetry—reinforce the theme of mutability: how we change and get used up but air changes and the climate (larger nature) stays the same. Even ecologists, I think, would not wish to argue with the poem's basic theme.

Another surprising move is taking place in this and in most of Edwin's poems: they are sonnets, modernized, yes, but Shakespearean sonnets nonetheless. In taking this tack, Edwin was going against the current of just about everything that was considered "advanced" at the time. (In a later, unpublished sonnet he wrote: "Aren't you ashamed to write sonnets / Of course, what are *you* ashamed of.")

In Public, In Private contains other shifts as well, from poem to poem: from rage and loathing ("A Sonnet Sequence") to spookiness ("Irish American Song"), from disgust for mankind ("The Poison") to humor ("Aaron" and "The Subway"), from contentment ("First Warm Days") to displacement ("In Salzburg"), from social alienation ("Elegy—the Streets") to warmth, friendship, and love ("A Postcard"). From the variousness of this book emerges the figure of a solitary, meditative man struggling to keep himself together and to see if he fits into the scheme of things—assuming there is one—and if we do.

These are poems to live with, to read over a period of time. The reader should expect them at first to be elusive, eccentric, or awkward, with a high density of thought. By reflecting alternately on their tones and meanings, however, one gradually acquires a sense of their wholeness, and the particular craft behind that wholeness.

In 1948 Edwin returned to Europe for two years on a Guggenheim Fellowship to write a book about contemporary European dance. (Although he never wrote the book, he did write essays.) He went via North Africa, visiting Paul Bowles for three months in Tangiers. After his longest stay heretofore in America—thirteen years—Edwin seems to have wanted a taste of a distinctly different culture. He probably needed the reassurance and refreshment of feeling out of place again, free of the heady but aggressive and competitive New York atmosphere. He was also curious about Moroccan life, "fascinated by the relationships between people,"[16] as he was fascinated by the relations between dancer and dance, sky and street, self and nonself. He was introduced to hashish by Bowles, but took too much and found himself, according to Burckhardt, wandering down some timeless hallway in his mind. Although Edwin had also once smoked opium with Cocteau in Paris, he never "used drugs" and was, after a brief romance with alcohol in college, a moderate drinker.

In 1949 his first volume of critical writing, *Looking at the Dance*, was published. Its pieces had been collected and edited by B. H. Haggin, with Edwin typically having little to do with it. Not only was *Looking at the Dance* one of the first, if not *the* first, collections of dance essays and reviews, it is still widely considered the best book ever written on the dance. Edwin, in Europe, was not present to enjoy the book's success.

His Guggenheim was extended for another two years after he fell ill and underwent an operation for a stomach ulcer. For some months after the operation he thought he was going crazy, only to learn later that mental disturbance was one of the possible side effects of the anesthetic.

During the peiod of his Guggenheim he traveled around Europe, and in 1951 he lived in Ischia for six months with the Burckhardts (Rudy, his wife Edith, and son Jacob). Together they toured Italy, Sicily, and Greece. It was in Ischia that Edwin met James Schuyler.

After returning to New York he met other poets and painters of the New York School: Larry Rivers, Jane Freilicher, Fairfield Porter, John Ashbery, Kenneth Koch, and Frank O'Hara. He was particularly close to O'Hara.

In 1955 he and Burckhardt went to Morocco and Italy for brief visits, which gave him the chance to put the finishing touches to the *Mediterranean Cities* manuscript. This book, in all likelihood written after 1948, was published with Burckhardt photographs in 1956. Apparently it received only one review, by Frank O'Hara in *Poetry* magazine in 1957 (reprinted in the present volume). In *Mediterranean Cities* the poet comes through not so much in what he says about himself as in what he says about things outside himself. From time to time there intrude suggestions of "uneasiness," "the crunch of anguish," "our unlimited dark," and "tearing grief," but there is no evidence that it is the poet who is feeling them; besides, the expression of such personal feelings is not the main thrust of these sonnets, in which the poet's sensibility is turned outward

---

[16] Gruen, p. 165.

toward the contemporary settings of what was in ancient times called Greater Greece.

This turning outward may have been an outgrowth of Edwin's work as a dance critic, which required that he focus his attention externally, see clearly without prejudice, and then write about what he saw. Not surprisingly, the infrequency of the "I" in these poems did not squelch the poet's presence, but made it more pervasive, as his sensibility is discovered not in the largeness of the self but in the largeness of the world.

There is immediate pleasure in the lushness of language in *Mediterranean Cities*, but also a complexity of syntax and meaning that comes clear only with sustained attention. In "Venice," for example, the first four lines are euphonious and haunting:

> She opens with the gondola's floated gloze
> Lapping along the marble, the stir of swill
> Open to night sky like in tenement hallways
> The footfalls, and middream a bargeman's lone call;

but the relationship of the clauses and phrases isn't obvious. What is doing the lapping? What is open to the night sky—"she," the swill, or the footfalls? The mysteriousness of relationships is even deeper in what might be called the second stanza (lines 5–8), which is almost cubistic in its displacements:

> Sideways leading to her green, her black, like copper
> Like eyes, on tide-lifted sewers and façades
> Festooning people, barges a-sway for supper
> Under hunched bridges, above enclosed pink walls;

The sense is clarified when one realizes that the "green" probably refers to verdigris, but even then the piling up of planes is dizzying.

Next comes an abrupt shift from cityscape to individual:

> And crumbling sinks like a blond savory arm
> Fleshed, a curled swimmer's pale belly that presses
> And loosens, and moist calves, then while the charm
> Subsides, Venice secrets pleases, caresses;

It is almost as if the city, the "she," had been making love, or had by osmosis become the swimmer making love to her, for the gender of the swimmer is not disclosed, any more than the particular kind of love-making going on. Something erotic happens. The experience subsides and we are returned to

> The water-like walking of women, of men
> The hoarse low voices echo from water again

where the poem began.

Venice's two extremes—its picturesque gondolas and its unattractive swill—are subsumed into its liquid, dreamy, sensuous, mysterious, ambiguously erotic nature, and we are left floating gently in its wake. The langauge does not merely provide an attractive description of a foreign place, it embodies the union of sensibility and place. This particular Venice cannot be experienced unless the reader becomes, for a moment, the poet, who has, for a moment, become Venice.

Just as the other places in *Mediterranean Cities* are not so mazelike and hermetic as Venice, the other poems in it are not so difficult. There are lighter moments, even some expressions of outright happiness, rare in so meditative a poet. (This is not to imply that meditation necessarily brings unhappiness.) The work is milder, less violent, more classical than that in *In Public, In Private*. The poems are permeated with history, but history taken personally, which enables the poet to give a richer sense of the way things are in any particular place. These poems are more public than private; or rather, the private is discovered in the public.

Edwin occasionally ventured beyond the sonnet form. "Elegy—The Streets" in *In Public, In Private* has its mate in the later "Snoring in New York—An Elegy." The latter was written over a long period, but exact dating is difficult, other than to note that the poem first appeared in *Locus Solus* magazine in 1962. On the whole it is more developed in theme and sophisticated in technique than its earlier counterpart, in which the pain of disappointed love drives the poet out into the street, where he seeks the consolation of society. In "Elegy" his rage is "but a dream." In "Snoring," on the other hand, his dreams are invaded by the sounds and appearances of people in the street, as he submits to "the advances of madness" along the borderline where sleeping and waking, anguish and gladness are interchangeable. The poem's language slides back and forth, too, between straightforward declaration and baffling ellipsis, with an undertow of sexuality.

This poem was published in revised form in 1974 with Edwin's last collection of sonnets, written most likely in the late 1950s and early 1960s. In these later sonnets (which Edwin never named) the rhyme has become looser, stanza breaks done away with, formality of tone left behind. The pace is quicker, the tone more personal, the mind more nimble. The sureness of gesture is comparable to the drawings of a master artist whose training and technique have become a part of his physiology, so that if his heart is true, then his line can never be wrong.

Edwin's later sonnets exemplify a wonderful balance between poet in the world and world in the poet. They are the poems of a man entering ripe maturity, with the richness of a whole life's experience, a poet writing for himself, with nothing to gain or lose by it, a poet for whom no idea is too large, no moment too small. For sheer attentiveness these poems are unsurpassed. The themes are those of solitude, loneliness, joy, astonishment, change, curiosity about others, kindness, anger, despair, death, the miracle of consciousness, and sympathy for the things of this world. The elemental power of places (New York City, rural Maine, Europe, the ocean) infuses daily life with a majesty and fascination that are also quite natural. Although in one poem Edwin describes himself as out of place, "an interloper," what resonates in these poems is an acceptance of this role.

In 1963 the special Edwin Denby issue of Ted Berrigan's *C* magazine appeared. Between 1963 and 1983 these other publications followed, none of them initiated by Edwin: *Dancers, Buildings and People in the Streets*, a second volume of essays, in 1965; *Mrs. W's Last Sandwich*, originally *Scream in a Cave* (1972); *Miltie Is a Hackie* (1973); *Snoring in New York* (1974); *Collected Poems* (1975); *The Sonntag Gang* (1983, in a special Denby issue of *Mag City* magazine). Some of these went through several printings and editions.

Edwin's sixty-ninth birthday was celebrated by a reading of his poems at the St. Mark's Poetry Project in 1972. To everyone's surprise, Edwin not only attended, he even read one of his poems ("Elegy—the Streets"), something he had always declined to do publicly. His reading manner was natural and conversational, his tone serious but agile. His reading made it remarkably easy to follow the contours of the poetry.

Dance magazine had given him its award in 1965. He attended the ceremony and even gave an acceptance speech, albeit one that trailed off. In 1979 he received the Brandeis University Notable Achievement Award. For the latter his friends had to drag him to the presentation at the Guggenheim Museum. Never before had the pagoda image been more obvious: Edwin, who was receiving the most prestigious award, sat on stage looking like an uncomfortable but luminous schoolboy as the other recipients made gracious acceptance speeches. When his turn came—the climax of the proceedings—he stunned everyone by striding stiffly to the podium and saying "thank you" and darting straight back to his chair.

His *Four Plays*, short dialogue pieces written for an Andy Warhol film that was never made, was produced in 1981 by the Eye and Ear Theatre in New York. Surprisingly, he attended many rehearsals and performances, taking great interest and delight in the production.

Although Edwin wrote little poetry or criticism in the last twenty years of his life—he kept revising his new pieces out of existence—his cultural life flourished. He could usually be found at performances of the New York City Ballet, Merce Cunningham, or Paul Taylor, and he closely followed the work of young choreographers of modern dance, as well as the many ethnic dance companies that performed in New York. He also frequently attended poetry readings by young poets. In the late 1960s he took an active interest in Robert Wilson's theatrical company, the Byrd Hoffman School of Byrds, and he never missed a show by painters he admired.

Edwin was very sociable. He enjoyed the company of his friends, with whom he dined virtually every night. He had a hearty appetite and a taste for good food. His conversation was brilliant, calm, and sometimes breathtakingly digressive (often causing some of his friends to regret that they didn't have a concealed tape recorder handy when they ran into him). As Frank O'Hara had written about him, "He sees and hears more clearly than anyone else I have ever known."

After 1965 he spent part of each summer in Searsmont, Maine, with Burckhardt and Yvonne Jacquette, the painter, at the rural house they all owned together. Across the road from the house are fields, a pine woods, and the big pond mentioned in Edwin's later sonnets. Not far away were other friends, such as Alex and Ada Katz and Neil Welliver. To Edwin's frustration, he couldn't complete a long essay on Burckhardt's work, which he had liked so much for so long.

A confirmed night person, he frequently went for walks alone around his (not particularly safe) New York City neighborhood, sometimes quite late at night, returning home alone to his cats. His slender build, silver hair, white skin, and blue eyes, his graceful manner, his attractive modesty, his inwardness, surprising in so public a man—all went toward giving him a kind of radiance, or spirituality. The book he read most in his last years was *The Divine Comedy* (*Purgatorio* and *Paradiso*—not *Inferno*) in Italian.

He bore the physical infirmities of old age with patience and even good humor, but what he could not bear was the disintegration of his mind, the onset of senility. On July 12, 1983, shortly after arriving in Maine, he sat down at a table, took an overdose of sleeping pills and alcohol, and left the world.

Ron Padgett

IN PUBLIC,
IN PRIVATE

THE CLIMATE

I myself like the climate of New York
I see it in the air up between the street
You use a worn-down cafeteria fork
But the climate you don't use stays fresh and neat.
Even we people who walk about in it
We have to submit to wear too, get muddy,
Air keeps changing but the nose ceases to fit
And sleekness is used up, and the end's shoddy.
Monday, you're down; Tuesday, dying seems a fuss
An adult looks new in the weather's motion
The sky is in the streets with the trucks and us,
Stands awhile, then lifts across land and ocean.
We can take it for granted that here we're home
In our record climate I look pleased or glum.

THE SHOULDER

The shoulder of a man is shaped like a baby pig.
It terrifies and it bores the observer, the shoulder.
The Greeks, who had slaves, were able to hitch back and rig
The shoulder, so the eye is flattered and feels bolder.

But that's not the case in New York, where a roomer
Stands around day and night stupefied with his clothes on
The shoulder, hung from his neck (half orchid, half tumor)
Hangs publicly with a metabolism of its own.

After it has been observed a million times or more
A man hunches it against a pole, a jamb, a bench,
Parasite he takes no responsibility for.
He becomes used to it, like to the exhaust stench.

It takes the corrupt, ectoplasmic shape of a prayer
Or money, that connects with a government somewhere.

THE SUBWAY

The subway flatters like the dope habit,
For a nickel extending peculiar space:
You dive from the street, holing like a rabbit,
Roar up a sewer with a millionaire's face.

Squatting in the full glare of the locked express
Imprisoned, rocked, like a man by a friend's death,
O how the immense investment soothes distress,
Credit laps you like a huge religious myth.

It's a sound effect. The trouble is seeing
(So anaesthetized) a square of bare throat
Or the fold at the crotch of a clothed human being:
You'll want to nuzzle it, crop at it like a goat.

That's not in the buy. The company between stops
Offers you security, and free rides to cops.

STANDING ON THE STREETCORNER

Looking north from 23rd the vast avenue
—A catastrophic perspective pinned to air—
Here has a hump. Rock underneath New York though
Is not a subject for which people do care.
But men married in New York or else women
Dominate the pavement from where they stand,
Middle-age distends them like a vast dream
While boys and girls pass glancing to either hand.
Sly Carolina, corny California
Peculiar Pennsylvania, waiting Texas
You say what you say in two ways or one way
Familiar with light-reflecting surfaces.
Time in every sky I look at next to people
Is more private than thought is, or upstairs sleeping.

A NEW YORK FACE

The great New York bridges reflect its faces
Personality scoots across one like tiny
Traffic intent from Brooklyn—it stays spacious
Aggrandized, in gales splendidly whining.

And adrift as figures on roof and pier-end
Stare at the gigantic delicacy, a face
So hangs its enormous ghost above the spent
Lover, too vacant for safety too still for sex.

In echoing darkness their dimensions become sleep—
River and dark neighborhood and skyscraper shape,
A hall-bedroom; faces all night inert in the leap
Of their fate so enlarge into grace without hope.

New York faces have a structure wide as this
Undisturbed by subway or by secret kiss.

CITY WITHOUT SMOKE

Over Manhattan island when gales subside
Inhuman colors of ocean afternoons
Luminously livid, tear the sky so wide
The exposed city looks like deserted dunes.
Peering out to the street New Yorkers in saloons
Identify the smokeless moment outside
Like a subway stop where one no longer stirs. Soon
This oceanic gracefulness will have died.
For to city people the smudgy film of smoke
Is reassuring like an office, it's sociable
Like money, it gives the sky a furnished look
That makes disaster domestic, negotiable.
Nothing to help society in the sky's grace
Except that each looks at it with his mortal face.

SUMMER

I stroll on Madison in expensive clothes, sour.
Ostrich-legg'd or sweet-chested, the loping clerks
Slide me a glance nude as oh in a tiled shower
And lope on dead-pan, large male and female jerks.

Later from the open meadow in the Park
I watch a bulging pea-soup storm lie midtown;
Here the high air is clear, there buildings are murked,
Manhattan absorbs the cloud like a sage-brush plain.

In the grass sleepers sprawl without attraction:
Some large men who turned sideways, old ones on papers,
A soldier, face handkerchiefed, an erection
In his pants—only men, the women don't nap here.

Can these wide spaces suit a particular man?
They can suit whomever man's intestines can.

THE SILENCE AT NIGHT

(The designs on the sidewalk Bill pointed out)

The sidewalk cracks, gumspots, the water, the bits of refuse,
They reach out and bloom under arclight, neonlight—
Luck has uncovered this bloom as a by-produce
Having flowered too out behind the frightful stars of night.
And these cerise and lilac strewn fancies, open to bums
Who lie poisoned in vast delivery portals,
These pictures, sat on by the cats that watch the slums,
Are a bouquet luck has dropped here suitable to mortals.
So honey, it's lucky how we keep throwing away
Honey, it's lucky how it's no use anyway
Oh honey, it's lucky no one knows the way
Listen chum, if there's that much luck then it don't pay.
The echoes of a voice in the dark of a street
Roar when the pumping heart, bop, stops for a beat.

PEOPLE ON SUNDAY

In the street young men play ball, else in fresh shirts
Expect a girl, bums sit quietly soused in house-doors,
Girls in dresses walk looking ahead, a car starts
As the light clicks, and Greeks laugh in cafes upstairs.

Sundays the long asphalt looks dead like a beach
The heat lies on New York the size of the city
The season keeps moving through and out of reach
And people left in the kitchen are a little flighty.

Look at all the noises we make for one another
Like: shake cake bake take, or: ton gun run fun,
Like: the weather, the system, the picture of his brother,
And: shake hands and leave and look at the sun go down.

One Sunday a day-old baby looked right at my eyes
And turned its head away without the least surprise.

FIRST WARM DAYS

April, up on a twig a leaftuft stands
And heaven lifts a hundred miles mildly
Comes and fondles our faces, playing friends—
Such a one day often concludes coldly—
Then in dark coats in the bare afternoon view
Idle people—we few who that day are—
Stroll in the park aimless and stroll by twos
Easy in the weather of our home star.
And human faces—hardly changed after
Millennia—the separate single face
Placid, it turns toward friendly laughing
Or makes an iridescence, being at peace.
We all are pleased by an air like of loving
Going home quiet in the subway-shoving.

ELEGY—THE STREETS

Si bien que si quelcun me trouvait au bocage
Voyant mon poil rebours et l'horreur de mon front
Ne me dirait pas homme mais un monstre sauvage.
Ronsard

You streets I take to pass some time of day
Or nighttime in the neutral open air!
Times when the rented room for which I pay
As if it could resent my mind's despair
Becomes like a trained nurse's torpid stare
Watching dead-eyed her feeble patient's malice—
When white walls feel like that, I leave the house.

Then, as dead poets did to ease their pain,
The pang of conscious love that gripes the chest,
As those men wandered to a wood grown green
And seeing a day turn grew less depressed—
Who long are dead and their woods too are dead—
Like them I walk, but now walk streets instead.

The public streets, like built canals of air
Where gracefully the foul-mouthed minors run
And fur-faced pets crouch at the side and stare
Till this one afternoon's one turn is done,
And animals and children disappear.
But all night the laid pavements remain bare.

Streets, with insistent buildings forced in blocks
Reverberating the work-morning noise,
With foolish taxis, heavy painted trucks,
Close-stepping girls and blankly confident boys,
With stubborn housewives and men of affairs
Whose self-importance looks jerky out of doors.

They pass in droves, detouring packing cases,
They press up close at crossings, dart at cars,
Some stop, some change direction, and their faces
Display unconsciousness, like movie stars.
The rage that kicked me howling in my room,
The anguish in the news-sheet, is here a dream.

The lunch-hour crowd between glittering glass and signs
Calmly displays the fact of passing time:
How the weight changes, now swells now declines,
Carried about for years beyond our prime.
My eyes—like a blind man's hand by pressure—learn
The push of age in the crowd's unconcern.

As comfortable as the day's pleasant thrust
That shifts the lunch-hour into afternoon,
So years shift each appearance people trust,
Deforming in detail—yet all, how soon!
The same years that in full view new create
Boys' agile backs, girls' easy-sided gait.

People pour past me in the summer blaze.
Each nose juts out, flat red tragic or high
Like a grove's leaves standing in different ways,
None like a monster occupies the sky;
My feature too that all my secrets sees
Stands here another nose, as used as these.

But in the night, in an avenue's immenseness
Emptied by winter wind and bestial sleep,
I like a dog alone then scan defenseless
The girder-trussed constructions near which I creep.
Dead as the limits of a person's fate,
As time one man can own, they isolate.

For property is private during night.
The passerby who glances up its floors
Pulls back his eye, meek as a hypocrite.
Up soars the facing wall, and up soars spite.
So fame impends, that mummifies and stores.
The fears a man has by himself are grand
Who peers about him where the buildings stand.

Grandeur that fakes the scale of my displeasure,
I who, one citizen, came for a stroll.
The fool who hates himself is not my measure:
I like the shell of streets in the cold's hole,
But not by pardon is my grief appeased,
By no humiliation, I, released.

This city and the piece between of heaven,
The stars in blackness on all the Atlantic Shelf,
It is the horrid birthright by birth given
For me to look at, who never views himself.
I watch in solitude the death of others
That splits my mind as children tear their mothers.

March moonlight wonders at this punishment.
The shine is mild and distances, unknown;
Flatly on cornices is the light spent;
The sky draws my eyes up, it dwarfs the scene.
I feel no need of hope that later ends;
I hate how rare it is to stay near friends.

So seasons alter the streetscape where I walk,
Illuminations its painted color use,
I stop for coffee, most persons like to talk,
They and I also long surviving news.
Interest awhile like weather will disperse,
I go back to my room and tie it down in verse.

A sound of measured language in the ears
In time, in place, wherever men inhabit,
Familiar tone within three thousand years
Verse is a civilized, a friendly habit.
Nature and money thrust us close, and sunder;
Verse makes less noise and is a human wonder.

A SONNET SEQUENCE: DISHONOR

Introduction

Happy in health not poor and with good friends
On the bright beach at noon I chanced to meet
The filthy double of me who attends
To secret matters I don't care to treat.

Repulsive and halfwitted that fine morning
I started to pretend I didn't know him
But he in fury with no word of warning
Stuck out his tongue to show me what I owe him.

His tongue licked up the sky that crumbled blackened
Sucked out my breath and peeled me like a shrimp
It stood up then majestically fecund
Death's own bisexual self-polluting pimp.

To him, his whore, these little dreams of hate
To get my honor back I dedicate.

I

I hate you, I feel your flesh suckling flesh
Here between my fingers the flesh I wanted to eat
All day all night sugary pink and white spin-mesh
I tear it rip it stamp my feet on it.

Sugary sugary I squeeze it full of dirt
Howling as I watch it spoiled for eating
A twin you floats up opposite intact unhurt
Pink and white smiling pretty to my bleating.

Fooled by a double ghost I heave and split
My dream finger from my dream eye but either
Was no part of the heart's solemn pumping meat
That blind by birth never can see dreams neither,

That goes on solemnly pumping itself through a fuss
While boiling dreams reduce the skin to pus.

I sit eating, from behind you put your orbed
Strong fleshy palm open over my head
I faint with love not recognizing you, absorbed
You twist it snapping it from the spinal thread.

Arms and legs of me grow rows of suckers, prehensile
Fasten on the pulpy swellings of your figure
Constrict blood flowing fresh, sucking stencil
You and burst your lung in a happy stricture.

One sneaky arm picks my head from the floor
Which has shrunk as small as an apple, and crushes
It sucking up the meat spitting this on your
Blackened but openeyed recognizable still luscious

Head, O your head, the picture of it inside me
Swells till I can't hold it till I can't hide it.

3

The words "once once only" are like weasels
I feel in my character, they frantically
Chew the bloody paste of memory where feasible
They filthily excrete in the part that's empty.

I can't kill them because they're fake creatures
And if I drop asleep they keep along otherwise
As huge obscure words watching me without features
Six of my love's fingers hanging out for eyes.

They trumpet their own names short and foul
And my love will shriek them dying alone
Once once only so it sounds like the howl
Of a horse drowning, his feet tied to a stone.

And watch their trick on this here paper how clever
They've festered on it presenting the word "forever."

They laugh when the fouled champion throws in the towel
They laugh when the gored horse stumbles in his guts
When the bulb breaks in the movie actress they howl
But never so loud as when a man loses his nuts.

And laughter being a token of happiness
Conclude what happy animals humans are
For an accident one imagines a real distress
When it happens rockets our pleasure way over par.

But the joy we feed our liquid blood with is dreaming
(A policed forest where lean hunters poach)
Bring home our love's face mangled and screaming
Or if we're the victim, looking at us in reproach.

This happy drug no public doctor cures us of
Each is a private addict to pleasures of love.

5

The married man is grateful for the stuffy room
That smells of his wife like a bar smells of beer
The eight-year-old child points with assurance to its home
Where grownups beat it, quarrel, and disappear.

The bald accountant back at his desk from vacation
Takes comfort in the president's angry order
The exile returning from honors in another nation
Feels a thrill seeing the first brutal face at the border.

The lover looks at them green in his despair
And his stomach ulcerates with selfpity
He is the only one who belongs nowhere
Even with money to pay his rent in the city.

A lover's home is in the facts of his dreams
Where he skins his love like a rabbit to his own screams.

As I cracked a pane I thought how I would like it
If I were cracking the convex pane of your eye
With a sledge in both hands heaving to strike it
Standing on a scaffold under a burning sky.

Do not look at a human eye from the front
The flesh curls around it and can ape,
But from the side you see it like a naked stunt
And any familiar hope is killed by its shape.

However I try to get at you you resist
Morsel of a body, black and blue
I could carry you around for years in my fist
A foreign thing and not domesticate you.

Horror that's held in the tidbit of an eye
And these disjointed thoughts, love will deny.

In an inch of forest violets are found
For an instant of ocean spray lasts
Large snowflakes readily touch ground,
This spell is the one my love's body casts.

Three people disputing do not change a slope
You can fool with a watch and the day grows
A cat passes the time without serious hope,
This truth my love's mind like a mirror shows.

My love's genius is other than accurate or rare,
Through two eyes the West Indian day spreads inside you
The moon on the dunes hangs up in the air
People show themselves and later hide too.

Love is the same and does not keep that name
I keep that name and I am not the same.

Three old sheepherders so filthy in their ways
Whores wouldn't touch them with a ten-foot pole
Saw once the Christmas star which in a blaze
Pierced like delight into the secret soul.

They later also stood with their same faces
Around a baby male and there were shown
The heart caressing with millennial graces
A beauty which in love is all its own.

These three were the first according to the story
But unbaptized they never will reach heaven
In an eternal hell tortured and gory
They can recall the joy that they were given.

This savage torture by the law of love
Of Christmas shepherds I like thinking of.

Here where a blank sky puts me at the center
Of how ardent a waste of land and sea
Where on all sides suns and moons leave and reenter
In a crowd of tides winds illuminations as if for me—

Where too for me the dunes savagely tufted and scooped
Are piled into mountains by a gnawing northern sea
Swaying they march on the forest, their armpits looped
With knotted pines, with turtles rabbits and chickadee,

Here in the middle of this dramatic tumult
I myself stand cast in the human part,
A stomach that grasps with a million cells at the insult
Rushing like nourishing blood from the void in the heart.

Proud of this world, eyes look at it and shut
Holding the vast inside firm as a nut.

The hot mist moves from right to left
Mixed with the sun like cloudy gin
The boy who now commits a theft
Pedals the bicycle of sin.

A nest of spring mosquitoes swarms
About the naked neck of thought
The spade that spades the sand for forms
Shows the store label newly bought.

And while I paint my vapid dreams
With liquid like a wooden house
My hand is dancing in the screams
That all day long blow from a blouse.

Mountain caress that telephone
That girls speak to each other on.

The day of thought walking in a day of sand
Holding in his hand a letter seven years old
A bunch of sand flies bites the exposed hand
The fingers of which a faded letter hold.

When blood, says the book, escapes by a secret issue
Drops and does not return to a gaping heart
The bleeding images dry with emptying tissue
Leaving the will as sand at last apart.

In the sand a wolf sits up on his hams like a dog
Presenting his filthy chest, narrow and fullgrown
He balances, his old eyes bloodier than a hog's
Look off, and his tongue lolls with a life of its own.

Like another time I gave in to death
I taste cinnamon on my breath, my own breath.

I had heard it's a fight. At the first clammy touch
You yell, you wrestle with it, it kicks you
In the stomach, squeezes your eyes, in agony you clutch
At a straw, you rattle, and that will fix you.

I don't know. The afternoon it touched me
It sneaked up like it was a sweet thrill
Inside my arms and back so I let it come just a wee
Mite closer, though I knew what it was, hell.

Was it sweet! Then like a cute schoolkid
Who does it the first time, I decided it was bad
Cut out the liquor, went to the gym, and did
What a man naturally does, as I mostly had.

The crazy thing, so crazy it gives me a kick:
I can't get over that minute of dying so quick.

Suppose there's a cranky woman inside me who
On the prettiest day rip! yanks down the window shade
But what a shade! no mote of light gets through
I breathe in pitchdarkness miserable and afraid.

She says she's Whistler's Mother. But I've heard her
Rollerskating down the hall when I'm sound asleep
Thundering in the dark and yelling bloody murder
She might as well be a subway I happen to keep.

At meals she eats like a wolf. Sometimes by mistake
Dives under the table and bites me too.
If I talk she makes noises like a hen or a snake
And if I don't she babbles, screw jew, screw jew.

She tore up your picture in one of her recent fits
But I felt around for and swallowed all the bits.

At noon the ocean like a sleeper breathing
Puffs out small breakers sucking them back under
A harsh and regular thrust that leaves a wreathing
Along the beach of dead bits of sea-wonder.

Gulls settle on the bars low water shows
Where dogfish die whose secret parts they sever
They squat for hours and foul the sand they chose
And with a strangled cry sail out forever.

On this bright beach all day I bathe and play
With light, and angry birds, and many colors:
Where a fly bites a drop of blood will stay
But standing on my hands can make me taller.

Past sunset in a corner of the beach
Perch jump for sperling and gulls dive for each.

The fragrant thorny island forest gleaming
Into an unseen cool and fragrant place
Deepens its growth from being into seeming
And the eyes spread themselves in deeper space.

Stereoscope both heart and eyes look through.
Just as they focus, mosquitoes get me, smack!
The forest flattens by a twist of screw
Into an inch and what was green is black.

This thickening black is some part of a landscape
Too close for any optical emulsion
So close the brain directly has to scrape
Its black pulp under an insane compulsion.

Happy compulsion! insane or back I thrive
This is love's flesh disfigured but alive.

Smelling or feeling of the several holes
Above the jawbone and below the belly
Suggests to searching lovers that the soul's
A slippery gumdrop filled with a sweet jelly.

A mouth tastes spicy like geraniums
Eyes like sweet trout, ears like snails to eat
And when it's lower down the lover comes
He's washed all through by something awfully sweet.

And though in the full course of his research
Each lover must deceive himself at will
Must falsify, forget, betray, besmirch
Debase and doublecross and nearly kill,

Yet licking their lips all lovers are agreed
The soul's a something very sweet indeed.

Thin air I breathe and birds use for flying
Over and through trees standing breathing in air
Air insects drop through in insect dying
And deer that use it to listen in, share—

Thickens with mist on the lake, or rain
Cuts it with tasteless water and a grey
Day colors it and it is the thin and plain
Air in my mouth the air for miles away.

So close it feeds me each second, everyone's friend
Hugging outside and inside, I can't get rid
Of air, I know it, till the hateful end
When with it I give up the insanely hid

The airless secret I strangle not to share
With all the others as others share the air.

A single person cannot talk so well
When no one answers where nobody is
What has a single person got to sell
Since all he has is singularly his.

Two people liking a like thing as two do
Talk buying and selling, close, and separate
Day passes through their house into a view
And doubly answered single sleep is great.

I who continue single sleep by day
And walking still see solitary black
With nothing to sell, with not a thing to say
Let night take me unnaturally back.

Close to that moment so my hope I keep
When after hearing last, I fell asleep.

A boy carries a light load. A grown man
Who breathes as easily one way as another
Seeing the boy forgetting, looking can
Recognize grace of a fallacious mother.

On a trail leading into a moist hollow
Deepshaded and dark, lit against the light,
A further glance the first illusion follows
Opening the eyes two ways by second sight.

But in the time when the mind's view is black
And cannot second the body's with perspective
When beaten up in a gangster attack
The strangled breathing of the brain's defective

Then, though scared to death by mugging trouble
The only thing we've lost is seeing double.

Break buildings, supper-sun in the sky
Buildings neither you nor I live inside
Break the table and the perfume on it high
In unventilated flats insiders hide.

Or during outside sunsets eyes open to see
An insider appears on the scene and acts
Six-thirty seven-thirty for you and me
Breaking, are not to him final facts.

He acts and his five minutes beginning back
With morning continuing unbroken light
Scares you and me stiff, so we guess we see black
And as he takes a step we know he's right.

Waiting forever for the next step, he breaks our heart
That no longer sees the street seem to break apart.

The street is where people meet according to law
Organize their natures to twenty-four hours
Say what to eat, take advantage of what they saw
And continue exercising daily powers.

Take one of these buildings, when standing awhile
The architect's headaches have been written right off
Just as a father's headaches amount to a smile
Like a cipher, when he gets the client to laugh.

So a million people are a public secret
(As night is a quieter portion of the day)
These are their private lives tearing down the street
Stepping past mouldings and past 'Special Today.'

Running they see each other without looking,
Love has not stopped, has not started by fucking.

AARON

Aaron had a passion for the lost chord. He looked for it under the
newspapers at the Battery, saying to himself, "So many things
have been lost." He was very logical and preferred to look when
nobody was watching, as anyone would have, let us add. He was
no crank, though he was funny somehow in his bedroom. He was
so funny that everybody liked him, and hearing this those who
had been revolted by him changed their minds. They were right
to be pleasant, and if it hadn't been for something making them
that way, they wouldn't have been involved in the first place.
Being involved of course was what hurt. "It's a tight squeeze,"
Aaron was saying in his bedroom, and let us suppose he was quite
right. He closed his eyes and shivered, enjoying what he did. And
he went on doing it, until it was time for something else, saying
"I like it." And he did. He liked a good tune too, if it lasted. He
once remarked to somebody, "Tunes are like birds." He wanted
to say it again, but he couldn't remember, so the conversation
became general, and he didn't mind. What was Aaron's relationship to actuality? I think it was a very good relationship.

THE FRIEND

Among the music, the shining flowers, and money
the heart goes on distilling hateful honey;
the family pass, the houses, foreign places,
the hungry heart asleep in soft young faces;
nobody knows what everybody's feeling,
the lifting eyes look out beyond the ceiling,
they see the damp, loved skin, they see it only,
the heart, uncertain, goes on feeling lonely;
and feelings leave, like morphia injected,
the sense of further spaces unaffected.
O sleep, most large of overpowering lovers,
and gruesomest of a heart's smiling covers,
O space of sleep, the unknown's intercessor,
the heart can swallow you, you are the lesser,
the heart has room to spare where sleep has glided,
it stands based on no bottom, easy-sided,
firm in no shape, clear wanting an intention
and far more casual than one cares to mention.

INDIANA

Mary went in little smiles
meant a little brighter
anyone without the piles
could frighten or delight her.

Ethel's mother makes the air
with peas and pins and panties
several boys were never there
giggling in their shanties.

I wonder if Father is coming,
I wonder if Father has gone,
strumming and thumbing and bumming
with an ice-cream cone for me.

Sister bought herself a squat
—could she have the knife—
hung her curtain cross the lot
at her time of life.

THE EYES

Love, your two great spheres of eyes
shining almost blue like stones
look as shocking as accident cries,
or on a walk like birds' bones.

Aren't you scared, too, to meet
—coming home before light break—
those globes of sense, wide on the sheet,
you have to twist through and then awake?

Love, putrid death won't tarnish
the blue glare of those lonely balls;
they'll lie around, kept in varnish,
two unsocketed incorruptibles.

ASSOCIATIONS

On fancy fronts of houses cracked but strong
light can accumulate the whole year long
and grow weed-like in the interstices
of faces rushing in and out of these.
How foreign is an eyeball beautified
by such a sprout that flowers from its hide,
how wet the secret, hidden like disaster,
that swells the root in either flesh or plaster
exploding down the busy street to view
in petals wonderful the whole year through.

This vista blurs, for pressing senses then
begin to shut the eyes, approaching men:
lapped in itself a baby that can speak
pleases with lovely fat that lifts its cheek,
or the fat grace of boys in puberty
like Winnie W and Hubert E;
more close at hand—like maybe geomancy
striking in both of us by luck and fancy
we please ourselves, till opening as they must
pleased eyes see nothing and the dark is trust.

Within the body like years beauty seeps.
The selfish pouting of a girl who sleeps
peculiar snorings of maturity
from living through us turn to what we see:
the astonished eye, assailed as from the rear,
sees what in front may love by love appear,
sees too those bits of blemish and of treason
which later rush and pop at human reason
inextricably fixed within its lens.
One world a whole and held is all it kens.

So in this nonsense cheerfully confused
the mountains linger easily diffused,
a season hangs a picture on a tree
and people look into the distance free,
things that are hidden stay that way today
and hear what all the others have to say,
the insects go about their hasty creeping
while in the house a boy and girl are sleeping,
a letter in the letter-box is seen
until they wake as evening widens in.

HELD

The bright young bones growing turn like green tendrils
but bright in the dark, but turning in slow young years
or like the bright flight of birds curving stilly
still almost and held by the mind's variable speed

In the mind's variable speed the young light body
and the green light hovering on fair sleeping hair
and the birdlike curve of too long limbs, wholly
held, turn in their slow darkness of yearning years.

LUNCHROOM

buoyed upbuoyed with pieces of familiar shoulders
fragments bear bear up fondly pillows warmly bear
and smoke and grey soft fleshly and carrying
and friendly muscles buoy near ignorantly
light breathing like bleeding feathers
in pores far at strange tables

IN SALZBURG

Fingers broke heavily a table-top, cold
the fleshfalls, skins displaced, baring kinks, frequent cut,
square, plane surface,
on forks, on tumblers of liquid, cheap, on news,
on peak, on backward,
feels the rollers for ill knuckles, bone-fit, side,
feels almost green color, like a nose, or a,
flings wet cloths, muffed through
for a chair leaned there heavy square table
weighing.

GROUPS AND SERIES

Suppose the morning light doubling with sense
the usual houses hiding residents,
and offered passing in a human eye
the pleasant sinews it is motioned by:
O shining cornea, the face's flower,
shine in the meaning of a morning hour!
O lower limbs, let enterprise afresh
shed lustre on the lovely eyeless flesh.

In enterprise, in sleep, how well men wear
the shifting illuminations of the air:
watching a sleeper we will come to trust
the body anchored in its breathing's thrust;
loosened in sleep, his weight lies there as such,
rounded in all this moonlight, cool to touch.
Beside you, broken by the lamp's short beams,
he shows you shadows black as parts of dreams.

In your eye's mirror, in the field it takes,
see next each shape the hole the shadow makes,
a hole that blurs, blots further like a flood
fed from the black that colors clotting blood.
Through the eyes' lentils thread this piece of death
until the hybrid lung draw easier breath,
contrary functioning superimposed
holds all our many senses safe enclosed.

O heart complete within a lovely place!
gathered, a sleeping beast, in private grace,
or playing like two dogs with other hearts
awake and eager, with barkdarting starts:
a word, passing unshattered through the ear
opens a further space of music here,
opens the days of love and all their stunts,
like views that hold all distances at once.

The day is bright with grass and tree and sea
partly entwined and partly floating free,
the shape of light plays with fallacious grace
in their relations, like a shining face:
it plays with you and me and yew and sea
and bee and be and I and eye and E.
And in this bright confusion we are bound
like anything to everything around.

LEGEND (AFTER VICTORY)

The bloated boy of nine lay on a shelf
After the war intimately smiling
In a cave among debris by himself
Alone he spelled aloud "Staten Island."

His cavern was at 55th and Park
Out of bounds for civilian personnel
Now he had slept off his drunk, in the dark
He knew if he lay still he could feel well.

He savored his profiteer mother's screams
Bereaved in her décolleté spreading her shanks
Like the screams the night when Army Hygiene
Had wiped out an infected area in the Bronx.

Those shrieks had made his spit taste of blood
The boy drew his assault dagger, he slit
The soft tip of a finger and sucked there good
His legs jerking in a spasm of delight.

Excited he slipped off his shelf, wary
Slid out through the rubble and hid watching.
A patrol approached. He seized a wrist, hairy,
And whispered "Mister" his child's voice catching.

In the dark in the unknown arms he sobbed.
His free hand unsheathed the dagger and struck.
He was kicked. A body scrambled. The sound stopped.
No scream. The boy cursed the unseen man's luck.

The boy lay in the stones shaking with rage
He couldn't kill in a world of grown men
He loathed the puniness of those his age
Inside he was a giant—age nearly ten.

ANOTHER LEGEND

A child singing to itself in the sunlight
Among the debris of New York likes a man's
Listening; and the other way round too is right;
Rarely, though in ruins, the two sing at once.
The gift either has is defenseless—pink
Of a child's mouth, repose of a man's hope,
Into the open day will vanish and sink;
Soldier and child, one drifts away, one vacant mopes.
Luck returns over and over in a long
Life. A child's beauty by electric light
Is muddied, but not theatrical song.
The President attends the opera tonight.
But death, listening in the wings to the painted
Singer, notes a weakness we take for granted.

ON THE HOME FRONT—1942

Because Jim insulted Harry eight years previous
By taking vengeance for a regular business loss
Forwardlooking Joe hints that Leslie's devious
Because who stands to lose by it, why you yourself boss.
Figures can't lie so it's your duty to keep control
You've got to have people you can trust, look at em smile
That's why we're going to win this war, I read a man's soul
Like a book, intuition, that's how I made my pile.
Anybody can make it, that's democracy, sure
The hard part's holding on, keeping fit, world of difference
You know war, mass hysteria, makes things insecure
Yep a war of survival, frankly I'm off the fence.
The small survivor has a difficult task
Answering the questions great historians ask.

MEETING IN THE POSTOFFICE

Was it you or myself I saw, white in the postoffice,
The white face hung in the air before the government marble—
Like the brutalized inmate who, questioned about his grievance,
Sees his own crazy face in the mirror and hears his speech garble.
A face, a face, mine, his, the President's, who cares whose face
Crazy alike, alike a horrible one-nosed lump,
The heart tied to the same known face of the human race
Goes into spasms of pain for a pet facial bump.
So we left that soapy government erection.
Dazed. Outside the day is filling the street and the farm
Equally. Heat and brightness and reflection
Play in the distance and in your look, doing no harm.
And now we coast like on the summer's crest
Seeing the east, and looking to the west.

THE POISON

Here the primped housewife has the choice between
Being vain of her provider or of loathing,
The smooth college-boy in his generous dreams
Quakes to think of himself in cheap clothing.
The rich man is in terror of being taken advantage of,
The intellectual stews his affection in envy,
The poor girl's bliss is to humiliate the boy she loves,
And the feeble try at least to cheat in their own family.
Therefore I hope the human species is wiped out.
But my shame is not a pang a billion people share—
Listen to them giggle and whinny and roar and shout
Look at them squeeze and feed and stare and snore.
Expecting little of themselves or others
Dying scares them, but to suffer hardly bothers.

IRISH AMERICAN SONG

Irish Yeats told of a barn, three men in there at night
One held a lock of hair up, two threshed by its given light
Did they know the woman whose it was? as remote as at a crime
The wan lock shone greenish and the men worked in that shine.
Here in New York where two or three persons lie asleep in a black
Room and the night lies in the airshaft on the bricks at the back
I know there is hair glowing like a weak bulb hung alone
But not what small manufacturing by its private light is done.
Young men with work, now lounging in a narrow luncheonette
In your underwear you get up from your bed without regret
Never will such a glow wake you at two in a hotel room
In the dead of night beside you, to use this monstrous bloom.
The fluorescence shed is like from my dead ma's radium clock
The man in the room with only a night his has his clock stop.
Tomorrow the people on the street will shine in the great light of
    day
Their bright young smiles will, which money gives and money
    takes away.

A DOMESTIC CAT

The cat I live with is an animal
Conceived as I, though next to me she's small.
More like each other, so our births assert,
Than either one is like a house, or shirt.
I nervous at my table,
She by the stove and stable,
Show what a gap lies between cats and men;
But shift the point of view to see again
Surrounding both of us disgusting death,
Death frames us then in this still room, each pumping breath.

Her white fur where she cleaned it smells like talc;
Her claws can tap the floor in a rapid walk;
Her shape in walking bulges up and down;
Jealous, she sits remote, but does not frown.
To sleep, she puts an eye
Upside down next a thigh
And lost the small snout grows a deeper pink;
To eat, above the neck her elbows shrink,
The outstretched neck, the head tilt when she chews,
They thrust, they gulp; and sated she rises to refuse.

Compelled, as men by God are, twice each year
Her look turned stony, she will disappear;
Exhausted, three days later, dirty and plain
She will creep home, and be herself again.
She cleans her young contented,
At one month they're presented,
Clear-eyed she hauls them out and on my bed;
Here, while they wolf her tits, she purrs, outspread.
She waves her tail, they look, they leap, they riot,
She talks. And later, when they've gone, she cowers quiet.

Graceful as the whole sky, which time goes through,
Through going time she wanders, graceful too.
Sits in the sun, sleeps rounded on a chair,
Answers my voice with a green limpid stare.
Modest in drooping furs
She folds her paws and purrs
Charmed by the curious song of friendly talk;
But hearing up the stair a stamping walk,
Under the bed she streaks, weakly disgraced,
As humble as an alleycat that's being chased.

We live through time. I'll finish with a dream:
Wishing to play and bored, so she did seem;
But said, she knew two kittens just outside
That she could play with any time she tried;
We went to see this thing,
But one hung by a string,
A kitten strung up high, and that looked dead;
But when I took it down, it was well instead.
All three then played and had a pleasant time.
So at war dreamt a soldier; for him I made this rhyme.

A POSTCARD

Elaine, Nini, Sylvia, Marjorie, Theda,
Each sends you happy wishes for your birthday,
Red and black Frances, Frannie, and Almavida,
Louise, gay Germaine too who is far away,
Kind Maggie, and Pit, Martha who prays gladly,
Jeannie, Ruth, Ernestine, Anne, Billie Holiday,
Husky Patsy, Ilse they love so madly,
And straightfaced Teddy—Dear Rudy, they all say.
And then Victor, and Bill, and Walter the mild,
And Frank, David, John, Aaron, Paul, Harry and
Virgil, the Photoleague, Oliver, Ebbie wild,
I and Gankie and the Shoe-man shake your hand.
Marieli and Susan come running at the end
And all of us send our love to you, our friend.

SONGS FROM LIBRETTOS

SONG

Abe, I need you, O Abe, so much
I don't know who I am, I don't know what I touch
The day like a furnace, the night like a stone
There isn't any sense in a woman alone.

I feed the chickens and I soak the beans
Stand with my arms adanglin' where the cottonwood leans
The days go by and I'm like outside
Watchin' them go, and wishin' I could hide.

I see the weeds shoot up, chokin' the crop
Choke it weeds, I ain't goin' to make you stop
Alive or dead, Abe's not ever comin' back
This is nobody's field, this is nobody's shack.

Why does a woman have to trust a man
Make a home for both like a woman can
One day he gets a notion out of the air
And he leaves the house as if he'd never been livin' there.

For a notion of his own, for a thinkin' whim
He throws away his home, it's nothin' to him
Where's a place now, Abe, where you and me can stay
Oh Abe, why have you thrown me away.

A man's heart is a hole that nothing'll fill
Fifteen years happy, it's treacherous still
No matter how he's loved you there's still behind
A lonely thought in a lonely mind.

I hate men, they're born to be alone
No woman ever had a man all of him her own
Leave mothers, leave wives cryin' out in their fright,
Yes, kill each other, you men, all you can do is fight.

SONG

Fate, fate of a kind no force'll tether
Loving and fighting for loving together
And a fierceness inside us that's big as life
Makes us one body like you could cut it with a knife
Together growing and again apart
Dying of loneliness and an empty heart
And again grown together and never alone
It's a beating in the mind joining dead and livin' bone
Strength from the living, strength from the dead
Strength from people unborn, that's the fate to which we're bred.

But here and now, you and me side by side
Sitting by a lamp with the dark outside
It's just us two and a single hour
Like two roots joined and widening out into a flower
Two sitting in the lamplight, don't know what's to come
But an hour stays true and a lamp stays home
Wonder of love that will not be afraid
To spring up in the dark by a light a man has made.

SONG

I don't know any more what it used to be
Before I saw you at table sitting across from me
All I can remember is I saw you look at me
And I couldn't breathe and I hurt so bad I couldn't see.

I couldn't see but just your looking eyes
And my ears was buzzing with a thumping noise
And I was scared the way everything went rushing around
Like I was all alone, like I was going to drown.

There wasn't nothing left except the light of your face,
There might have been no people, there might have been no place,
Like as if a dream were to be stronger than thought
And could walk into the sun and be stronger than aught.

Then someone says something and then you spoke
And I couldn't hardly answer up, but it sounded like a croak
So I just sat still and nobody knew
That since that happened all of everything is you.

SONG

Ain't you ever noticed with a girl or along with a pal
How there's a big country inside them you never get to know
Like at night in the hills you hear two kids that call
Far off, far off from each other, and never no more.

Or like at another time above the canyons you stand
And the sun is bright on that country like on promised land
And maybe behind you where your cold shadow is thrown
Are other canyons in moonshine, the unknown you yourself own.

Land so large you never travel out of yours into his
View so far a lightning flash can cross the abyss
Miles on miles in that basin how small a town appears
Look, how small an act, action, done among the desert of years.

All this is our country. Pride is this country inside
Pride the view as over our own, view beyond over others as wide
Open boundary we are born with, like the undefended breath
That makes us here the same as brothers, and equally
      separate in death.

When you look at night at a stranger beside you in sleep
His breathing body lays there right under a common sky
Wide open to the dark is the common greatness bodies keep
We all live, live great and defenseless as you and I.

SONG

Sure we're different, and none of us the same
Some got better looks, some got a English name
Some hold their liquor, some hold their wife
Take your turn, and have the time of your life.
No use thinkin' you're better than the rest
You don't believe it when you get undressed
Come down off the grandstand and join the old parade,
We're American anyhow, hell, of who are you afraid.

Some like to do the shoutin', let 'em go ahead
Keep your shirt on, they'll stop when they're dead
God how they rile you, it's a fact they do you dirt
Cheat and boast of it, that's the big shot kind of squirt
Looks like the best way to keep money in its place
Is graft a couple of angels on the human race
It's plain unreasonable how the rich folks act
We're American anyhow, and that's a fact.

Everybody knows how everybody lives
The trouble it takes, and the glory it gives
Wash the spinach, tidy up the home
Catch a freight, and roam, Romeo, roam.
We all start young, later on we're old
And most of the time, boy we do as we're told
If we work in the sun or we work in the rain
We're American anyhow, from California to Maine.

When you seen the moon on the roofs of the rolling freights
You get a feeling it's our own, the whole United States
It's one wide country and there's lots of us in it
Like we say free and equal, like we keep trying to begin it,
A feeling we're sure of, and a secret we keep
No use gabbin' up and down and makin' it cheap.
So what? So it's plain as the nose on your face
We're American anyhow, say, all over the place.

SONG

When you're sitting at a counter or in a grocery store
Talking to the Greek, and looking out the door
And *he's* remembering some goats, and *you're* killing time
And there isn't any business in his or your line
Nor pretty sunshine
So you have here a tomcat on your knees
The local tomcat settled on your knees
And he's looking in your face and he's bothered by a sneeze
And he's purring like an old Model T with a wheeze
Mrrr mrrr chiff mrrr
Well,—he can't help but widen out and curl in his paws
Through your pants he pricks your knees with his claws
You blow smoke in his face but it don't give him pause
He's so pleased with himself and so pleased with you
Lying stretched out in your lap like it's the place he grew
He's a New Yorker who feels good through and through
And doing nothing in a grocery is a satisfactory thing to do.
Oh Mrs. Blatt
If you wasn't you you should be a mother cat.

I saw a lunchroom kitten on the tile in the sun
Stretch all four legs out, and then lift its head, yawn
Then fold itself together in a private little heap
And there in the middle of the world go contentedly to sleep
And all alone in the world go contentedly to sleep.

SONG

Twenty years way on the East Side
Where the investigator prowls and the dummies hide
Where the janitor is fit to be tied
Ride her, sodajerker, ride.

Sit on the River, sit on Tompkins Square
What you see of the weather is the same as anywhere
Wherever you sit, you're always there
Take care, Bud Mac Doc and Pop, take care.

Mama, what you got to eat, to eat
Standin' with a bunch of kids in the doorway up the street
Come up off the street, get out on the street
Neat (*whistle*) that's how they get me, neat.

You're a family man, he's a family man
Never got the point of it, but that's what I am
It's a long time ago that we all began
Hey, dope! Can you take it? Say, we can.

SONG

I have a secret
Maybe it's wrong
I have a secret
All my own
I don't tell it
To anyone I see
Because I only know
It's true in me.

There was a girl
Far far away
And she was I
How small she looks today
She had a secret
I remember it too
She loved Miltie
She didn't tell but it was true.

I remember one day
I knew it was so
I knew I loved him
Oh it seems so long ago
Like all of me knew it
True in me as I
Mine, and forever
And so the years have gone by.

And I have a new one
I know it now
My own today
I hold it unshown.
Only for me
To own like I know
Not to tell but love
And, like a secret, grow.

Grow to be terrible
Like the question: Life or death?
So this air I breathe
Can be, oh, my last breath
Grow so it blots out
All I know but I
Till there is no more truth
Only will we live or will we die.

I wonder at the many women
Who have been—ah—mothers
Can it be I shall be
Later only another?
I watch and I wonder
Was it once all in all
And years have gone by
And they see it so far and so small.

A lie, a lie, that's a lie
I know now, yes I know
The day I have is a secret
All around me while I go
And all the days to come
All my life till it may be born
I own them, they are mine now
The future, large as fright, is all my own.

How much more I know then
Than Mary with her sweet first scare;
I think of Susan, when she was seven months gone,
How she walked with oh such care.
And I think of Miltie
How honest and good he is
How happy I am to have him
And the baby I have is his.

POEMS WRITTEN TO ACCOMPANY PHOTOGRAPHS BY RUDY BURCKHARDT

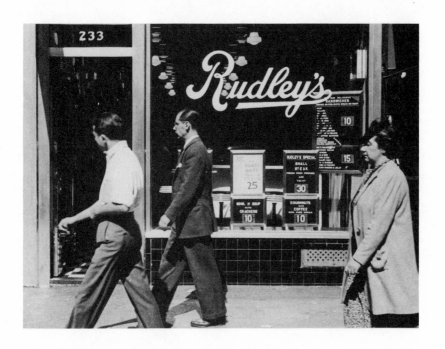

ADJOINING ENTRANCES TO OFFICE
BUILDINGS IN RENAISSANCE STYLES

Post factum our fate is causally blue-printed
To palliate its ridiculous immensity,
Our architecture also instead of demented
Is viewed as a function of our own density.

The solemn face of a banker at breakfast
Smiles at his wife (and at his girlfriend at the office)
As this sweet stone pastry set in the jambpost
Curls back (devoted) from the building's orifice.

But the lines go on forever like us
And the screwy angle to the pavement is the same,
A few words make a longer hush
We touch each other, and a name, a name.

(Dinginess, insanity, immensity, and use
Are the lozenge projected from the square of these views.)

LUNCHEONETTE COUNTER DISPLAY

Professor: What is advertising and what isn't?
Answer: Magic is a joke you pay cash for.
Do you want to be refreshed or not be refreshed. Listen,
We study savage psyches, and these please more.

A commercial artist is a dreamer, don't worry,
He says when he says he means it he means it:
Take a girl, it's got to happen in a hurry,
And when it's once pointed out you've practically seen it.

Pictures count ten, a word alone a million,
And plenty more where they come from, brother,
All right, a spookbusiness, it don't kill you,
It's our living space where we can love each other.

"Isn't it frightening," says the professor's wife.
"As much, Madam, as humanity's mental life."

MID-DAY CROWD

When they build for a million a day to use it,
What is the point in, say, five hundred years,
Abroad they've still got the pyramid of Whoosis,
Would it last in New York? The answer is, who cares.

So many a day makes anything like forever:
So a hydrant is (the joke is on the designer)
So the shutter of a camera is open forever,
So how's the fuckin wife, christ, couldn't be finer.

Isolated, active, attractive, separated,
Momentary, complete, neat, fragmentary,
Ordinary, extraordinary, related,
Steady, ready, harried, married, cute, astute, hairy.

Created equal as they say, so where's the pity?
In a split second a girl is forever pretty.

NORTHERN BOULEVARD

The bench, the sewermouth, the hydrant placed
On the street are attractive and foolproof,
Their finish is in republican taste
The expense, on democratic behoof.

People wear the city, the section they use
Like the clothes on their back and their hygiene
And they recognize property as they do news
By when to stay out and where to go in.

Near where a man keeps his Sunday plyers
Or young men play regularly, they place
Next to acts of financial empires
An object as magic as a private face.

No use to distinguish between hope and despair
Anyone's life is greater than his care.

LAUREL HILL

A desert is fine for engineering
You use it and shack up on top of it
New York that might have nestled endearing
Fixed itself a desert on which to sit.

At Laurel Hill, Greater New York City,
See the soil Fifth Avenue encases—
Ground for a mining camp, base for meaty
Three-year-olds with free, impervious faces.

See the chapel like a blueprint. A skyway
And a graveyard. The light is so clear it cuts.
Being Sunday, the truck is home for the day.
With a drink at the radio pa sits.

Far away is right here on a plain sky
Air anywhere to change, anywhere to die.

FIVE REFLECTIONS

I.

Hung Sundays from Manhattan by the spacious
59th Street Bridge are the clear afternoons
In Astoria and other open places
Further in the enormous borough of Queens.

Thickly settled plain an ocean climate cleans
Rail and concrete, asphalt and weed oasis,
Remote Queens constructs like desert-landscape scenes
Vacant sky, vacant lots, a few Sunday faces.

In this backyard of exploitation and refuse
Chance vistas, weights in the air part and compose—
Curbs, a cloud, metropolitan bulks for use
Caught off guard distend and balance and repose.

So New York photographed without distortions
Show we walk among noble proportions.

2.

Meeting a freightyard head-on, the wide street
Heaves its surfacing on steel, takes to the air
Handsomely ponderous, expensively neat
Crosses the property and descends with care.

Along the sidings plants stand white and square
A rooftank on their innocent concrete
Like a pod; steel-filigree masts, sunk and spare,
Power high across the track-area secrete.

These utilities, clear as a toothbrush
And whose unmoveableness terrify
Suspended here in a photograph's hush
Contact and reciprocate the spread of the sky.

Even like a modest look on a large face
See the bolted lattice-work have almost grace.

3.

On weedy outskirts the factories lodge
As casually as tents that nomads dispose—
A few men loafing in front of a garage
Have a look like it of uncommitted repose.

And so despite the divergent windowrows
Concrete flatness and its white resplendent edge
The eye looks for how the ground's undulation goes
Undomiciled, taking the sky for a gauge.

Evasive looking, coexisting with police
With deeds and contracts, with paychecks and bills—
These are the views a heart finds to beat in peace,
Like the country of years it once only fills.

The eyes play with the luck their limits contain
Caressing a slender lamp-post, a squat sedan.

4.

You can have the measurements O.K.ed, mailed,
Talk with the bank, and get the building faced,
Carry it on the books, and when the firm's failed
Pedestrians still go by the slabs as placed.

Pride shifts from this accomplishment to that,
Leaves old killings and half a city built,
The noise that smoothed it like a swimmer's fat
Disintegrates into Sunday bits of dirt.

Measurements however in straight angles to
The pavement and a standpipe do not so move,
As if the mind shifts slower than people do
And keeps widening the space between love and no love.
This widening like a history mystery
Is what Rudy's camera takes in the city.

5.

An eye is wide and open like a day
And makes a sign in an American field,
The field of lettering, which reaches each way
Out to the section-line and does not yield,
Stops simply at that imaginary line
That begins a like life in a like square,
A neighbor's other name and other sign,
From here (like) you can see Ray's silo over there.

Rudy like Sherlock with a microscope
Finds this field under our nose outside the heart,
But says he wasn't thinking of farms, the dope,
Nor of the charm of the inscription part.

(In the mind, though, this enormous intersection
Moves about like in water a reflection.)

To peer at the common man as at a hero
Is an error like addressing Hitler, Hey Mack,
As a man of the world your rating would be zero,
All you get from Mack is a view of his back.

Believe it or not, this city is common
To people who are historically unsuccessful,
Any day anyone is no other than someone,
A woman can be particular and a man full.

Some place any one is someone anyday,
Which Rudy proves here clearly out of Euclid,
Or any one is no other than someplace anyway—
Leaving a dictator as an historic nucleus,
Someone today is anyone in the same place,
Not to his family, but like considered in space.

In the eighteenth century, which was not long ago in Italy, Naples was the third city of Europe, the most extravagantly noisy, dramatic, poor, and happy of all. A big maze of lofty slums, palaces, and churches, huddled close together in narrow alleys, is still alive from that time, and very much alive. Whatever else they are now, these slums are still of all slums the happiest and kindest. They are Naples.

Poor or not, each city proud of its name chooses its own particular kind of luxury and has it. That of Naples is to have the brightest, prettiest, and happiest children; the most everywhere underfoot too, mixed up in everything that goes on, up at all hours, quickwitted, graceful, each one different from all the others and perfectly sociable. Knowing everything does not make them any less innocent, any more than it does grownups. For them grownup life is all the time a wonderful dramatic show, with the most unexpected jokes and exciting surprises. And for grownups the children are all the time—or nearly all—a sort of angelic and impish ballet. Sunny Naples lives by the delight of children.

As long as they can just as well be underfoot, there is always room for them to play. If the slum is nested in an old palace there is a grand courtyard. Or in a tenement building—a tenement is called a palazzo too—there is a small court, where for the benefit of his serious-minded cousin, a curlyhead can make a brilliant proposition or a striking entrance. Or else there is the street, so narrow that machines can't squeeze their way in and squeeze children out, so that the small open squares among the narrow alleys stay free too for children and chickens. The two little boys in the alley are helping mamma by lugging the chairs downstairs and out to the pump to be washed. The young man with a hoop has a solitary poetic thought. And here the whole neighborhood has seen that a photographer has come. Take me, take me. And again here in another neighborhood. What choreography they invent. Ancient Naples has chosen the sweetest luxury of any city.

MEDITERRANEAN CITIES

TRASTEVERE • A DEDICATION

Dear head to one side, in summer dusk, Olga
On her terrace waters potted azaleas
Thoughts of friends, their fine successes, their failures
Greek reliefs, Russian poets, all water with her;
The plants rejoice; across the street, the high wall
Reaches the decayed park of a long dead Pope
Urchins stole the sphinx near the fence up the hill
Where woods grow thick, sold it to a Yank I hope;
Now young priests smoke at the basin, by blurred sea-gods
Above them rises a hairy thicket of palms
That male in their joint green dusk yield Rome the odds
Returning with the night into primeval realms
As laughing Olga, feeding through the window cat-shadows
Then reading, then sinking into slumber, too does

VENICE

She opens with the gondola's floated gloze
Lapping along the marble, the stir of swill
Open to night sky like in tenement hallways
The footfalls, and middream a bargeman's lone call;
Sideways leading to her green, like black, like copper
Like eyes, on tide-lifted sewers and façades
Festooning people, barges a-sway for supper
Under hunched bridges, above enclosed pink walls;
And crumbling sinks like a blond savory arm
Fleshed, a curled swimmer's pale belly that presses
And loosens, and moist calves, then while the charm
Subsides, Venice secrets pleases, caresses;
The water-like walking of women, of men
The hoarse low voices echo from water again

RAVENNA

A governing and rouged nun, she lifts the cubed
Jewels, garlanded heavy on hair, shoulders
Breasts, on hands and feet, the dark-blue the cell-roomed
Splendor's fountain lifts sunken to Him Who holds her;
But the emperor is running to his pet hens
Cackling like a hermit, and his foolish smile
Alone in the vacancy of noon-glazed fens
Haunts a blossoming water-capital's guile;
Holy placidity of lilylike throats
Ravenna of fleets, silent above the cows
A turnip plain and stagnant houses floats
Exultance of sailor hymns, virginal vows;
In a church's tiered and April-green alcoves
Joy rises laughing at ease to love God's loves

FLORENCE

Delicious tongue that poisons as it kisses
Arno, that Dante guzzled sandy and hot
Licks streets glummer than New York's but possessing
Capacious idols dead magicians begot;
Graceful as the idols, glancing limbs and fingers
Swaying bellies thread the streets, liquidly proud
A kissing of observant flirts who tingle
Dangle like brass ornaments on a used bed;
Beyond the hospital, slopes of soft olives
A prospect of humped tower and of floated dome
Shapes in the confined landscape where August seethes
Wasting, present Tuscan violence untamed;
Alurk, the hillocks, a dwarfed peak, a shallow plain
Peasant like Arno, lie insidious in the blaze

SIENA

Lost in cool small sane hills an immense sea shell
Palaces drowse around its void, jockeys swirl
Far above a shaft adolescently swells
To stiff blossom, a tower like a still girl;
Stone hollow, luxurious as memory;
Fine-boned, the feeders at Byzantine messes
Catherine's blood people, in corners of an eye
They stroll cool and joking with Duccio faces;
In her darkblue shell, Mary, by coppery angels
Exalted, warily heavy she retreats
On her picture, comes forward like a heaved bell
The fat pearly Son frowning into the surf-beats
Of my heart, till where an overwhelmable shore lies
Citied, in almond-blossoming foam, deep-sea selves rise

ROME

Pear-brown Rome, dyed for the days whose blue is sweet
Disencoils as a garden would the wreaths and noses
Waists and loose fountains it adores to prodigate
A fair-weather darling as loose as roses
Soft up to the scar, dead Imperial Rome's;
But an American in the exposed ruins
They meet him like a face unrecognized from home
The mute wide-angle look, to Europe alien;
A stare of big men worried about their weight
Gaze of bounty, but too clumsy to have mourned
Or held, listening to the heartbeat which was a fate
Sky-hues that will return, the slope of solemn ground;
And I to whom darling Europe is foreign
Look home from here, to its mystery, with longing

VILLA D'ESTE

Beneath me this dark garden plunges, buoyant
Drops through the trees to basins furtive below
Under me wobbles the tip of a mast-thick fountain
I laugh and run down; the fat trunks heavily grow;
Then cypress, ilex rise reflected immense
Melancholy, and the great fount thrusts forceful
Tiny, their seclusion perches over the plains
For plains billow far below toward Rome remorseful;
But rilling streams draw me back in, up above
To the spurt, dribble, gush, sheath of secret water
Plash, and droves of Italians childish as love
Laughing, taking pictures of laughter, of water
Discovering new fountlets; so dense, so dark
Single on a desert mountain drips the locked park

VIA APPIA

Roman, the narrow road in a brown plain
And freaking the grass undercut heaps of brick
Turdlike shapes or fungoid, that are tombs by name
Ruined Roman tombs famous as picturesque;
Stalking the undulant expanse, legs piecemeal
Of dead aqueducts, discolored by distance; close
A farm; by a parked scooter a couple quarrel
Intently, standing in stillness anonymous;
The solitude has the face of an actor who
Sits in his wrapper and hears silence return
But not yet vanity; so giddy, so free
As if one were dead, were dead, the heart becomes;
At dinner with lively friends, drinking Tuscan wine
In Rome that night, how I loved the restaurant's shine

VILLA ADRIANA

Who watched Antinous in the yellow water
Here where swollen plains gully, Roman and brown
Built for fun, before a flat horizon scattered
Fancies, such advanced ones, that lie overthrown;
Urbanely they still leer, his voided surprises
Curved reflections, double half-lights, coigns of rest
Embarrassing as a rich man without admirers
Peculiar like a middle-aged man undressed;
Over the view's silent groundswell floats a field
Enskied by one eerie undeviating wall
Far to a door; pointing up his quietude
Watchful Hadrian exudes a sour smell;
The ratty smell of spite, his wit, his laughter
Who watched Antinous smile in yellow water

OLEVANO ROMANO

Samnite, such a high hilltown made Romans cross;
Viewed below, April ledges of grape or rye
Slim greens, deeper green in the valley, and a voice
Chanting on the mountainside; Dante woke too
To dawn of rain, thrush, of farmers' and beasts' tread
Leaving the cold alleys tight about the keep
Driven diurnally from the mountainhead
Down to farm, at dusk resorbed upward to sleep;
They sleep close; clouds like hounds coil on the mountaintops
And the bare Spring, girl-like Olympian hunter
Sharp for our smell, shudders; so old the night drops
While people lie flaccid and covered grunters
Godless; a dream stirs one, she scents them again
And they flee like hares through wide delight and close pain

NAPLES

I feel of night streets as of a reef, squamous
Grotto-wash; entombed, claws loose, a Siren lies
Who bleeds, the phosphor-drift leaps in these Naples
Eyes, thousands of eyes, thousand and one night eyes;
By day, a crater; the oldest the island
Ischia, a solitary shire in an
Illuminated sky; stinking springs, birds silent
Oblique speech where is sand or a hoed vineyard;
For between volcanoes Naples tattered shelves
Loud dense mother sudden in adoration
Among children who hop among her themselves
Deck her screaming in variegation
Each a spell or a carnation
Pensive, when she calls like the moaning in a lie
Parthenope's lascivious guttural cry

SANT'ANGELO D'ISCHIA

Wasps between my bare toes crawl and tickle; black
Sparkles sand on a white beach; ravines gape wide
Pastel-hued twist into a bare mountain's back
To boiling springs; emblems of earth's age are displayed;
At a distant end of beach white arcs piled
Windows, and in the sea a dead pyramid washed
As if in the whole world few people had survived
And man's sweetness had survived a grandeur extinguished;
Wonders of senility; I watch astonished
The old hermit poke with a stick the blond lame boy
Speaking obscenities, smiling weird and ravished
Who came from New York to die twenty years ago;
So at a wild farmer's cave we pour wine together
On a beach, four males in a brilliant weather

POSITANO

In the sky the mountain hunches blindly forward
Hugely falling crowds close, and a caverned head
Grovels between foam; from blackened lips of shore
Grinding, the waves with snake eyes forever evade;
Averse sea, small on it a far swimmer died
Small in his skull a mother was calling, goatherds
Drunken pranced among boats, the orange branch, light
Of a streetlamp over the breast of a betrothed;
The mountain dropped him from its breast; rosmarin's
Savage scent, an arching deep gorge, purple cliffs
Pink and yellow sky, sea-sheen with their sweets enspin
The hunched hugeness, the mountain of groveled grief
Jealousy falling forever inward unlike ours
A gigantic phantom fed on by men and flowers

AMALFI

In flowered cliffs she crouches, by a remote strand
Candid Amalfi, of boatmen's burning eyes;
Down the peaks a tempest plunges, flood yells, drowned
Screams from alleys, then a dripping and warm skies;
Altered, the throaty voice rising sinuous
Caresses, antique look deeper than a kiss
Melting, the longing body smiling like a face
Sidles heavy-curved; and gratefully it lifts its grace
As in citizen dusk groups strolling witty
Provocative meet foolish eyes and sweet; a Pope
Old Briton, found the honor here as pretty
Eight hundred years ago, who watched without hope
Widen the sea, lilac below his palace
That far in storms Amalfi's hearts would swallow

PAESTUM

Buffalo among fields, an old bus, the sea
Rock hills grow small beyond a somnolent plain
Jacket folded placed near the bole of a tree
Between a jug stood and a wrapped package lain;
In the sweet alyssum and its honey smell
Noon-immobile, grey and ochre-hued like dawning
Of edged stone pocked by sea storms and shells of snails
Poseidon's hall looms columned; I watch dozing
Merged like opposed wrestlers rear a majestic power
Clasped nape, nipple deep-chested, the crushing roof
Heaved; magnanimous the god rises toward me; prayer
Begins to spread me, trembles unused to proof;
But by sunset fired against a cloudbank of slate
And deserted, the temple burns isolate

SYRACUSE

Are you Russians the boys said seeing us strange
Easy in grace by a poster with bicycles
Soft voices in a Baroque and Byzantine slum
Lemon pickers by swelling seas rainbow-fickle;
On the height drizzle, and among thyme and mint
A small shepherd, a large canvas umbrella
Leaps away down the crumbled ruins, timid
Where once they fought in moonlight, and Athens fell;
Up in sun, the Doric fort, stone blocks graceful
And fresh, erect as a statue in the air
Bright wind in our eyes, bright sea glittering peaceful
The dead come close trusting to embrace, and glare;
Beyond where rode an American fleet, Pindar's
Snowy Etna, pillar of Sicily, blows cinders

SEGESTA

Winter's green bare mountains; over towns, bays
And Sicilian sea, I sit in the ghost stones
Of a theatre; a man's voice and a boy's
Sing in turn among the sheepbells' xylophone;
From a distant slope sounded before a reed pipe
Sweet; a goatherd, yellow eyes and auburn down
Smelling of milk, offers from a goatskin scrip
Greek coppers, speaks smiling of a lamb new born;
Doric tongue, sweet for me as to Theocritus
The boy's mistrust and trust, the same sky-still air
As then; so slowly desire turns her grace
Across the years, and eases the grief we bear
And its madness to merely a powerful song;
As the munching boy's trust beside me is strong

TAORMINA

Under orange groves from a winter sea rising
With winter roses, towns, vineyards rising slow
Rising massive with run magma, black slag shrines cling
To, the black screes, and the voidly soaring snow
Etna cloud-overbillowed, Etna in sun
Pure in the moon, huge diaphaneity
Phantom nearness, though nightlong burn in unconscious men
Dreams, and incandescence roars below the sea;
Rose bud, I love your pout, love the ash-built slope
Rising rising, the sea beneath me, the sea
Where in curls like these sweet in my hand a coast
Enjoys its shape and turns embraced, Sicily
Hard roses swelling, remote hills wild and steep
Lifts to a father's mouth lips opening in caressed sleep

FORZA D'AGRO

Leaving the bambino home, by bus, afoot
Past a wild sea-keep, we climbed to the viewed town
Got lost among pigs, at last unguided stood
Above roofs, steeps, the sea, under Etna in rain;
Cold poor town, more beasts live in it than people
Was their joke as the young priest showed us paintings
Who when I urged a hot-water bottle giggled
And took us to the cafe where all was wanting;
The gangster from New York was building his house
But sweetly priest and a youth leaping showed the path down
We ran down lost in sunset to make the bus
And in a black winter night got safely home;
The lithe girl watching her goats, sparkling and fifteen
Smiles her clear smile as sleep and tearing grief return

BRINDISI

Where nervous I stand above nocturnal ships
The Appian road ends with one pillar at the shore
Ghostly Greece whispers in the waves' lapping lips
Lips Vergil heard here, sweet Vergil dying in despair;
The old woman who sees him sleeps in that house
By his boots she knows him, his long white coat
He foretells lottery numbers, courteous
But she don't win she says, she don't read numbers good;
Harbor, lost is the Greece when I was ten that
Seduced me, god-like it shone; in a dark town, trembling
Like a runaway boy on his first homeless night
Ahead I rush in the fearful sweep of longing
A dead longing that all day blurred here the lone
Clear shapes which light was defining for a grown man

ATHENS

The traveling salesman helps me on the subway
To a Ritz in Union Square; up Levantine streets
I recognize afar the actual display
Of the Parthenon, a brown toy in morning light;
In noon whiteness I find Ilissus' trickle
Past tennis courts and refuse; plane trees
Shade the concrete bed, planted for Plato's sake
At girl scouts drilling a man through a fence peers;
I hop a bus, "Academy," a boy fourteen
Looks deeply at a soldier, we reach a flat slum
A desolate vacant lot; Colonus is seen
Past factories, rising stony from the plain;
Ghosts I have brought with me smile at my discomfiture
Joyous they touch their dear city, laugh in its dry air

THE PARTHENON

The keen Propylea spread like a male hand
Grey rock glints as with violets, on the height glows
Heavy-foreshortened like a body's grandeur
Womanly, the Parthenon, yellow as a rose;
Desert blue of Attica's heaven; white light
Like an intent silence enjoys the languor
Secret in her dominion, the intimate
Smile within holiness, droop in her candor;
Delicious her Ionian companions
New laurel wreaths at the fluted column's base
Their straight pure walls beside her ample clear ones
Her maturity duplicit like a richer kiss;
She lifts from men dead into my passing life
A beauty of doubt that is homeless and not brief

ATTICA

Spaciously outdoors of cafes Greeks put chairs
Set way across a square or a bare road, roomy
As if huddling weren't the point of architecture
They remain present; so Greeks sit firm, ungloomy;
So a small house has a temple's paint; flowers
Individually blooming in the stone landscape
Firm in brightness, bloom with a deeper color
Heavier fragrance than at home a namesake;
And deep blue as violets blooms the Protean sea
Heavy-petaled in the noon's inclusive delight
Blooms among mountains, beaches bare afar and dry
Peaks keen in shape, islands lucid and afloat;
There on brown Egina this light broke a Roman heart
Vergil's, whose voice comforts in our unlimited dark

MYCENAE

By a gorge, the height where Clytemnestra slew
Scrub grows in Mycenae, a triangular
Peak above it and slow slopes outrolled below
Wide to majestic summer, Arcady afar;
A lintel in the grass, crimson stone; no walls
That remember; Rudy and I dark in a tomb
Speaking of the pompous Pantheon we smile
Cool underground we smoke in a sphere-curved room;
But the gorge, like a hole hacked furious in haste
At possession, gapes under the royal height
Grandly; and no need has a forgiveness; lost
We turn away to the parched plain, the desert light
To our friendship; under Greek oleanders
Blooming white in the brightness downward we wander

THEBES

High Cithaeron where Oedipus cried lies bare
Diluvian from in a plain rise cone-shaped hills
Two, far off as Thebes; uneasy through the glare
I watch them swell, step back; suburb, the bus jostles
And mounts; gone the wall music built, Amphion's;
We enter Thebes past a Frankish tower, a shed
Of diggings, a clinic by American grants
Built; the painted street at noon stands wide and surd;
Reserved Thebes, a country town; after sunset
Wild-eyed, ragged in the crowding dusk a boy
Holds out silently for sale a toy acrobat
Daubed paper; I peer, take it with sudden joy;
On the Hudson in a room that branches brush
It lies on a table, hears the crunch of anguish

DELPHI

Heat on the majestic flank of Parnassus
Blazing noon; sunsick we reach beyond ruins
Cold Castalia's source; watered farm horses
Wait in shadow, a man sleeps dark near the spring;
Above the cliff eagles, olives shimmer below
Mountain opposite, then deep the sea-plain, mountains
An airy ease rustles in this high beech grove
While outside on white plinths snakes make fulsome stains;
Through July noons the Pythoness snoring drowsed
And Plutarch conferred shaded; no fright is here
Where the unseen vent a thousand years was housed
And a stooled hillwoman shrieked to men in prayer;
Her pulpy moving tongue spoke truth, majesty
Is its vestige in the mountain peace we see

DELOS

Dark pure blue, deep in the light, the sea shakes white-flecked
Foam-white houses sink, hills as dry as dried fruit
In a gale, in a radiance massive like sex
The boat bounces us and Greeks in business suits;
A thick-built landing stage; an isle low and small
And one old hill on it, cake-shapen; screening
Her solitude other islands bulge and sprawl
She lies dazzled, floating, as remote as meaning;
Left among the Hellenistic marble scum
Glistens a vivid phallus; marsh-born here before
At a palm, cleft-suckled, a god he first came
Who hurts and heals unlike love, and whom I fear;
Will he return here? quickly we pluck dry flowers
The sailor blows his conch; Delos disappears

MYKONOS

Brown bare island stretched to July sailing winds
At a beach houses blinding as snow; close-by
A warren of curved white walls; families within
Marine, the women, the girls are strict and shy;
On the saint's eve, the square where they danced was small
Like a Greek loft in New York; between candles, chairs
A slow row moved stocky in the night sea-chill
The saint's neighbors, the rest of the town not there;
In a bare room, like a sailor's few souvenirs
The sacred objects—vowed small church that mates build
Cold during winter—all-powerful Christ repairs
As Son to such a table and sweetness is fulfilled;
The rose like our blood in its perishable bloom
Sweetens with remembrance a white unlocked room

Flying from Greece to see Moscow's dancing girl
I look down on Alba Longa, see Jacob's house
And the Pope's, and already the airplane's curls
Show St. Peter's, and the Appian tombs' remorse;
But Jacob, a two-year-old American
Is running in the garden in August delight;
'Forum not a park, Forum a woods,' he opines
In November quiet there on days less bright;
Now in New York Jacob wants to have my cat
He goes to school, he behaves aggressively
He is three and a half, age makes us do that
And fifty years hence will he love Rome in place of me?
For with regret I leave the lovely world men made
Despite their bad character, their art is mild

CITY SEASONS AND SNORING
IN NEW YORK

CITY SEASONS

The winter that now comes with light and height
Holds all New York in its contrary might
Black every face and stone against the sun
Like paper flowers tall buildings shone upon

Once the stove gets to heat the quiet loft
Returning from the street, my thoughts are soft
Aware how redhaired Jimmy never came
And how cat Marieli loved to hear her name

Pictures by Valdes, by Rudy, by Bill
My home with heroism and friendship fill
And the illuminated city shines outside
In ocean wind and beach-far eventide

2.

The spring goes drifting, angel of deceit
Touching the towers' ledge with rosy feet
Descending to the sidewalk flower-soft
And letting float like a balloon my loft

In uptown streets the clothes grow light and quick
The taxis foolisher, the eyes more sleek
Persons who hated, meeting by chance they smile
As if insidious spring should reconcile

Dear angel, carelessly you make us bloom
More clear than ours, more transient is your doom
And grateful as a cat I take your stroking sweet
That mews and rolls in my nocturnal street

3.

Mothmouth and Butterfly live in my loft
Dancing and hunting, feline friends and soft
Loose in noon-heat collapse, but the night-wandered breeze
That brings me rhymes, adventures brings to these

The blazing sun of August sweeping wide
Burns open secrets that a heart would hide
"Arthur" the loyal, brother of beauty "James"
Of treason and of filth become the names

Blue as of Venice stands the morning sky
By night the buildings bloom, resplendent, high
Drunk as Li Po I watch the yellow moon
Remember pleasure, remember what comes soon

4.

Colored autumn long ago vanished unheard
Raspberry afterglows viewed from Twenty-third
Bluish mist midtown as in ruins of Rome
Forest mornings in Manhattan, my home

Streets as of stone empurpled, insect traffic
Of a fall remembrance keeps fantastic
Over lilac haze Indian summer sky
Spread its azure as if nothing would die

Those fall mornings I woke to make tea
Talk to a cat, find the silence of a new day
Were crazed; they have left and here is winter
Winter's white sun and nocturnal glitter.

SNORING IN NEW YORK—AN ELEGY

When I come, who is here? voices were speaking
Voices had been speaking, lightly been mocking
As if in and out of me had been leaking
Three or four voices, falsely interlocking
And rising, one or two untruly falling
Here, who is here, screaming it or small calling

Let it call in the stinking stair going down
Mounting to a party, the topfloor ajar
Or later, a thick snowfall's silence begun
Crowded boys screaming shameless in a fast car
Laughing, their skulls bob backward as if weeping
These happy voices overhang my sleeping

I slide from under them and through a twilight
Peer at noon over noon-incandescent sand
The wild-grown roses offer warbling delight
Smell of dwarf oaks, stunted pines wafts from the land
The grin of boys, the selfcentered smile of girls
Shines to my admiring the way a wave curls

Or just their eyes, stepping in washed cotton clothes
Tight or sheer, rubber or voile, in the city
Hot wind fanning the cement, if no one knows
Noon-incandescent, the feel at their beauty
Stranger's glance fondling their fleshed legs, their fleshed breast
They enjoy it like in a pierglass undressed

And enjoy the summer subway bulge to bulge
The anonymous parts adhesive swaying
Massive as distortions that sleepers divulge
So in subterranean screeching, braying
Anaesthetizing roaring, over steel floors
Majestically inert, their languor flowers

And nude jump up joking alert to a date
Happy with the comb, the icebox, the car keys
How then if rings, remark or phone, it's too late
Fury, as unpersonal as a disease
Crushes graces, breaks faces, outside inside
Hirsute adults crying as fat babies cried

Covered over, lovered over and older
The utterance cracked and probing thievishly
Babyfied roving eye, secretive shoulder
The walk hoisted and drooped, exposed peevishly
The groom's, bride's either, reappears in careers
Looking fit, habitual my dears, all these years

So at the opening, the ball, the spot abroad
At the all-night diner, the teen-age drugstore
Neighborhood bar, amusement park, house of God
They meet, they gossip, associate some more
And then commute, drive off, walk out, disappear
I open my eyes in the night and am here

Close them, safe abed, hoping for a sound sleep
Beyond the frontier that persons cross deranged
Anyone asleep is a trustful soft heap
But so sleeping, waking can be interchanged
You submit to the advances of madness
Eyes open, eyes shut, in anguish, in gladness

Through the window in fragments hackies' speech drifts
Men, a whore, from the garage, Harlem and Queens
Call, dispute, leave, cabs finish, begin their shifts
Each throat's own pitch, fleshed, nervy or high, it leans
In my open ear, a New Yorker nearby
Moves off in the night as I motionless lie

Summer New York, friends tonight at cottages
I lie motionless, a single retired man
White-haired, ferrety, feminine, religious
I look like a priest, a detective, a con
Nervously I step among the city crowd
My private life of no interest and allowed

Brutality or invisibility
We have for one another and to ourselves
Gossamer-like lifts the transparent city
Its levitating and ephemeral shelves
So shining, so bridged, so demolished a woof
Towers and holes we sit in that gales put to proof

Home of my free choice; drunk boys stomp a man who
Stared, girls encompass a meal-ticket, hate fate
Like in a reformatory, what is true
To accept it is an act, avoid it, great
New Yorkers shack up, include, identify
Embrace me, familiarly smiling close-by

Opaque, large-faced, hairy, easy, unquiet
The undulant adolescents flow in, out
Pounce on a laugh, ownership, or a riot
The faces of the middle-aged, dropped or stout
But for unmotivatedness are like saints'
Hiding no gaps, admitting to all the taints

They all think they look good—variegated
As aged, colored, beat—an air unsupported
But accustomed, corpulent more than mated
Young or old selfconsciousness uncomforted
Throw their weight—that they each do—nowhere they know
Like a baseball game, excessively fast, slow

Mythically slow or slow United States
Slow is not owned, slow mythically is like dearer
Two slowly come to hear, one indoors awaits
Mere fright at night, bright dismay by day, fear is
Nearer, merer and slower, fear is before
Always, dear always is, fear increases more

More civilization; I have friends and you
Funny of evil is its selfimportance
Civilization people make for fun; few
Are anxious for it; though evil is immense
The way it comes and goes makes jokes; about love
Everybody laughs, laughs that there is enough

So much imagination that it does hurt
Here it comes, the irresistible creature
That the selves circle until one day they squirt
It lifts sunset-like abysses of feature
Lifts me vertiginous, no place I can keep
Or remember, leaping out, falling asleep

LATER SONNETS

Out of Bronx subway June forest
A blue mallard drums the stream's reach
Duckling proud crosses lilyleaf
The thinnest of old people watch
And Brooklyn subway, Apt 5 J
Dozen young marvelous people
A painter's birthday, we're laughing
Real disaster is so near us
My joke on death they sweetly sink
Sunday follows, sleepy June rain
Delighted I carry icecream
A few blocks to friends' supper drenched
Baby with my name, old five weeks
I hold after its bath, it looks

New York, smog-dim under August
Next Sahara-clear, the Park trees
Green from Chelsea, then blinding gusts
Of grit, the gale, cloudburst increase
Europe, that you've not got, weather
The manners, gondolas, the walls
Restaurants, hills, noon, dusk, friends there
Sweet Europe, you're so comfortable
But differently spread close asleep
Stagnant softness, oppressed secrets
On your breath, thick-throated Europe
Uninnocent masterpieces
Nudged, I wake dressed, seated writing
New York cat asks, Play with my string

Neighbor sneaks refuse to my roof
Cat snores—that's a winter landscape
Newcomers shining in the loft
Friends' paintings—inattention to cope
With the rest—the tap's voice, the street
Trucks, nextdoor coffee, gas from drain's
Hole, the phone's armorplated speech
Snow's hush, siren, rain, hurricane
Nature crowds, big time, into, out
The building and of the man I'm
I do with nature, do without
Penetrated, also sublime
I'd like the room mine, myself me
But as facts go, neither's likely

Born in my loft, dancer untame
A wilderness imagined, small
Cat, which we reached for real by plane
You stalked on the roof up the hall
Heart nursing six kittens, that grew
With them, long-tailed splendid-eyed cat
A disease struck the womb, left you
Savage fighter, playful at night
Lamed, ireful you prowled then; vet cut
Out the womb, so rage might subside
Telephone rings, speaks, I hang up
Cat-heart that knew me gone, I cried
It stopped beating drugged in a cage
Dear, mine will too, and let go rage

Cool June day, up the avenue
An oldster in a boater steps
Jaunty, at the cross-street, light green
Steps out, truck turns in on him, he stops
Truck halts, the driver don't crowd him
Midwest highschool kids of his own
He'd spotted the gait, gives pop time
Lets them honk, soberly waves him on
Old man couldn't move; a PR
Touched the arm, smiled, walked him across
He took up a stride like before
Traffic regained momentum lost
Irish like the President's dad
We watched him swallowed by the crowd

Slight man walking, inveighs to himself
In Spanish, old frump does, English
Trucks, taxis roll, loud relief
Self listening to unlistened speech
Imagined answer awaited
Like the moon's reply, the bayed moon
Satellite, it shines belated
On New York, where we rest unknown
Rest after the reply of fate
To each specific without weight
But weightily sweethearts on edge
Caress their voices or quarrel
Before knowledge, after knowledge
Fondle both voices, boy's and girl's

Writing poems, an employee
I lived here at nineteen, who I?
Current boys nineteen, their beauty
Of skin, all I can recognize
On this passport, soft vague boy's smile
Recalls few facts, does, his horror
Scale's abyss, void becoming real
A heart's force, he was going mad
Which I?—surviving forty years
Schizophrenia of a goof
I remember his savage tears
The kind reproof, the kind reproof
Vague-faced boy, he faced what was it?
A white old man, approved, I sit

Alex Katz paints his north window
A bed and across the street, glare
City day that I within know
Like wide as high and near as far
New York School friends, you paint glory
Itself crowding closer further
Lose your marbles making it
What's in a name—it regathers
From within, a painting's silence
Resplendent, the silent roommate
Watch him, not a pet, long listen
Before glory, the stone heartbeat
When he's painted himself out of it
De Kooning says his picture's finished

Great man's birthday, my face continues
The others, wrinkled, smooth, here too
The dead politely diminish
Infants, the unborn press nearer
Equally enviable, more, less
These, those, each so different from I
Imagination in and out rushes
Vulture stranger, aswoop the sky
Drunk on champagne in the street we
Throw snowballs, embraced shout for soup
Quarrel, vanish, brilliantly speak
Each as close to death as a dope
From a birthday go to my bed
Which unpresentable is spread

Small paintings seen, I cross the Park
Toward six, end of March, pellucid
Close boulder, black velvet so dark,
Glare, one or two lithe descend it
Grass March-green, in air the hard buds
Flushed barely the buildings' vista
Up Fifth, downtown is where I head
Scraps of Park speech, blown scraps of paper
Equably whole sky fades coldly
Streets welcome dusk's private thought
None wide enough to hold you in
Happy to the subway I trot
Caress of a March afterglow
Of its color this much I know

The winter nights sat through, it's May
Ocean of light at two o'clock
Theatre darkness, lit ballet
Small trees aflower, Central Park
I smell blossom, tot clicks toy gun
Couples embraced kiss, families eat
"Strike Two," Maytime satisfaction
Near my shoe sparkles dark granite
Vacant, bend and touch it, bed-rock
Below blasted, my neighborhood
Nightly, the arclights on its bought back
Manahatouh's glens, it has stood
Cell-mess and million-yeared Hudson
Petrified has grudged their motion

Translucent white, straw-brown, or grey
The ocean sandgrains spilled on a palm
Ocean, ocean's round atmosphere
White dune at noon's incomplete calm
Or greenish star-scape, shack lamp-lit
The night, the size unseeable
Far roar, near hoot, crunch underfoot
Storm-dark or moon fog instable
Leaving that return to New York
Millions of persons, one a world
Outside and in, now light now dark
And food paid for, belief whirling
Each as much as I the center
Walk, phone, recognize and banter

Slight PR, tiny son, she lay
A drunk Irish on pavement
WASP, my block, heave her upright
"Two bucks, the bastard," bloody trickle
Steer her one each side, he's relieved
"She my building," his child trails us
Honest Christians, lurching we go
She heavy every which way, groans
Steep stair, he pushes her ass, she quickens
Grocery bag take from brown tiny hands
Return to my door, my five flights
At home can't recall anything clearly
Except small boy's bright eyes keeping his face straight

Sunday on the senator's estate
Eleven of us shoot a movie
Seven drive home at one a.m.
The driver awake among sleepers
Yellow full moon, July New Jersey
Smog meadow, eight-wheelers festooned
Merging rise, toll, tunnel curving
Manhattan night, inbound, outbound
Imagination nobody
Does without, it hurts so and laughs
As if not you, not I will die
The world vanish, vanish knowledge
Who's to support me, you phoney
Be hostile, slob, get the money

The size balls are saddens Lamarck
It's of no relevance to Marx
And Freud shoots his lunch at the fact
Dad's funny if he's just as small
July subway, meditate on
The decently clothed small male parts
Take the fabulous importance
Felt by homes, felt better by farts
They won't be missed, science will soon
Claim, parthenolatric more than
Religion, women left alone
To travel planets with women
In the lit subway gently shook
Imagine they've a goodbye look

The grand republic's poet is
Brooklyn Whitman, commuter Walt
Nobody else believes all of it
Not Harvard, that finds him at fault
I have, but first he broke my heart
He points to the moon and breaks it
I look for him, Twenty-first Street
Sleep against the push of a cat
Waking stumble to start coffee
At my back Walt in underwear
His head slants from unaltered day
Strokes my cat, the cheeks streaming tears
Sits on the bed, quietly cries
While I delay turning round, dies

Grey blue ridge, grey green leafage
Lucid Maine, a Laborday hush
High goldenrod, slope dun, spongy
Field that alder and pine-bush broach
I watch glitter the woods, watch budge
The underfaces of branches
Forest holes on which my eyes bed
Obscure voids that my heart munches
Against nightsky black nature humps
Below the edge makes a dense mess
Fern, fox's bark and my bed lumps
To inches joint of namelessness
Sentiment shot, sleep I will trust
In pre-shadow dawn-light adjust

Cold pink glowing above wakes me
Sky-light, ok, it's dawn, cat wants out
Outdoors I see skysea of pink
Blue pine bush, lightbrown goldenrod
Dazzle like baby cheek and hair
For acres, for miles of country
Each exposed brute so pure, so clear
Coolly on earth as in thought's joy
Me too, old man who pees adoze
Then dressed rereads Dante's Eden
One of dignified culture Joes
Lots of them take walks in Sweden
A me, free of himself at dawn
Sleeps, this me reads in noonday Maine

Heavy bus slows, New York my ride
Speeds up, on the hill Rudy waves
Then faster seize me, pivot, evade
A mien, step, store, lawn sliced from lives
A nap at dusk; entering night
Landscape threatens, no matter which
Caveman's faith, artificial light
A shack in the woods, the turned switch
One a.m. stop; drunk or sly strangers
Turnpike, the bus wheezes, slows, drives
And so Bronx, known Manhattan kerbs
Turned key in my lock, the door gives
Miserably weak, pour some shots
Don't look, make the bed, it's day out

New Year's near, glass autumn long gone
Daily done tasks that required it
Like a no-trouble office man
One undone, scale from which I shrink
In my clean loft with the heat on
It's fifty, zero outside, gale
Banged sash, gust screams, gust-rolled ashcan
Tonight the two stray cats here wail
I can't tell them the facts of life
The Cuban bomb, or cats in snow
But a ribbon takes their mind off
Fall asleep twined, later with me
Two, three nights, weather becomes soft
Awhile, and cosier my loft

Awakening, look into sweet
Beast eyes, nightmare dispelled, cheerful
I feed cats, me, do chores; the great
Day waits then for heroism
Exhausted, I get myself out
Store, gallery, chat, have coffee
Heroes, heroines abound; hope
Who trusts it, but it's contagious
Back upstairs, poetry I try
Alive by chance, civilian I
Chance roommates, you cats and roaches
You have cultures purer than mine
Of yours I shelter the success
And at mine's failure don't repine

Inattentively fortunate
Have been pausing at lunchcounters
While what I most like, art that's great
Has been being painted upstairs
No homebuilder, even goofy
To virtue have been close as that
It I love and New York's beauty
Both have nodded my way, up the street
At fifteen maybe believed the world
Would turn out so honorable
So much like what poetry told
Heartbreak and heroes of fable
And so it did; close enough; the
Djin gave it, disappeared laughing

Disorder, mental, strikes me; I
Slip from my pocket Dante to
Chance hit a word, a friend's reply
In this bar; bare, dark avenue
The lunge of headlights, then bare dark
Cross on red, two blocks home, old Sixth
The alive, the dead, answer, ask
Miracle consciousness I'm with
At home cat chirps, Norwegian sweater
Slumped in the bar, I mind Dante
As dawn enters the sunk city
Answer a one can understand
Actual events are obscure
Though the observers appear clear

Nocturnal void lower Fifth, I
Stepped in that desert off the kerb
A roar spurting eighty whams by
What a pleasure, I wasn't killed
Laughed how dear the morose asphalt
Tail light at Sixth, waiting for a green
I'd recognized it, a friend's car
That like enraged had roared past me
Game unmentioned when we met, roar
Obscure he, I, have let alone
New York accommodates years more
Daily the unknown and the known
Sometimes I can't, madly gloomy
Recall that events are roomy

Jacob, thirteen, sends me wishes
From Rome—he and Rickey shivered
Swimming in Maine—for a sixtieth
Birthday which I will have survived
Remote that September-smooth lake
By airmail more than winter Rome
The scarves, snow, sharp sun, smiles, graces
Jacob from school in the bus home—
Half-grown male and full-grown eunuch
The cats rough-house, chase each other
Bother me, deep in the Pentateuch
At two a.m., beasts of Eden—
He knows this loft, sloping and white
Jacob wakening, now I'm in night

Since freshman spring intimate, his
Face—mysteriously well known
Like a forest—here by jet, speaks
To mine, that I can't imagine
Older woman or man alone
Lights ablaze dozes, farts, is drunk
Unregards night, wonderful one
Overflows like a rifled trunk
Marvelous seasons that last long
And return to shut street, farm-scape
Don't correspond, do, to the pang
Now much slower, now much quicker
Events I know, of which I write
Without Homer's adequate light

Roar drowns the reproach, facing him
Quite near, subway platform, she heeds
Head tossing slow like a pony's
In the wrong, the pinto I rode
A boy of twelve, that lovely head
Quarrels I believed riders win
White-haired pass these lovers in luck
Hurry to ballet, its invention
Where there's no quarrel, but there's fate
A scream unhurried of music's choice
And we recognize the games played
Like in heaven, foreknowing they cease
The move, the pitch arrive, turn to air
Here, as if love had said forever

Drenched saw Doris home, midnight gale
Later a hospital weak Helen
At five, coffee oatmeal alone
Dark Union Square, me light-headed
Two youths lope sullen, one; flood-lit
Penthouse, me walking to my bed
Walk cautious as if drunk up Sixth
Prowl car walk past at my corner
The night's end foreknown, furred roommate
Witty neuter with his beast fate;
White-polled like my ghost grandfather
Reads in my sleep dreadfully
The grandeur of scene, of persons
Frequent safety, random city

March warm on matinee Broadway
Faces flattened by glare like dung
Vicious or vicious by hearsay
The primped elders, the self-drugged young
Friend fair in a clinic, I stride
Hurrying to a play's preview
My face equally falsified
Buys a ticket to see what's true
No use, outdoors surpasses in
Steak's price spent, the rush-hour subway
Bodies close as married, not seen
Accommodate each other, they
My home block, now late afternoon
Upstairs quiet, one, I alone

August heat; night hail; mute freshness
Moon stormclouds, purple, Turneresque
Delight Rudy; done in, still dressed
Sleeps Yvonne, in bed sleeps Jacob
Time passes; white moon-soaked mist
Solitary outdoors, book indoors
Dear careless moonlight, dear dead words
I know them near, feebly I drowse
Ghost from inside of me, peevish
My mouth hardens at your approach
Figure incomprehensible
Of happiness not reached and reached
Sleeping hunched upstairs, Tom-baby
Year old, when he despairs, rages

Drought has burnt the meadow pink-gold
At night the long black house hutches
Dropping asleep these colors glowed
It's morning, Tom whimpers, clutches
Morning; a neighbor drives by, waves
Chainsaw in woods, barks distant dog
Green hills, a bug, the near leaves
Sunny field, gloomy forest edge
Where loom forward its withdrawn presences
Pitch-green, glittery, than ours older
Their sort soul, millionfold animate
Noon Tom sleeps, later eats mud at the pond
Proud as a president toddles on the road

The meadow rolls slanting like the
Heave of a midocean wave; woods
Ensecret a mossgrown road, path
To our lake, the land a neighbor's
Shoes on grass, I slow in noon's silence
Step by step reach the water blindly
The torments of weakness disgust
They're so unreal, everyone kind
Greedy my soul upsidedown leaps
Into the deep sky under me
A more brilliant autumn it swims up
Rising inside the lake's mirror
It leaps back, ribbons of color
Impenetrably beautiful

Bright and light the wooded country
Bright and heavy the small lake, over
The hills are others though not seen
The sky shining on their water
The morning sky is so pale, it's
Early, in it clouds float shallow
Deep up, it becomes like brighter
Near the horizon, yellowish
Opaquely the windy water
Glitters, branches, the weeds before me
Translucent, leaf-green the far shore
Woods, that fir-boughs blue-black intersperse
The tokens of a vanished forest
Whose shade secludes my hope's darkness

Cold dew, forest trees silenced
Disused field in a corpse-faced dusk
Shack black, low full moon, go inside
Like exhausted remain awake
Wrapped in blankets, hear throb a jet
New York friends sleep in the nightscape
Under trees their cars, August yet
Arboreal shadows, moon-cast
Moon-drawn Maine hills, roads, lit window
Child's cry, wife's laugh, the continent
At peace, darkness don't walk into
Evil expects wit I haven't
It's reached me; puff my candle's light
Unnoticed globe, unnoticed night

Leaves between trunks spreading far up
A green spray among high needle boughs
Darker than before the forest
Down here seems when I look back down
Dark boughs and trunks, myriad scribbly twigs
Recesses flecked with shine, with color glows
Silence crunched underfoot, detritus
Mushroom, a root-claw, mosses, underwood
Squatting, the floor's hummocky rot
Dead needle and leaf rug, each's edge, tiny
Dry, bacterial like my mind's clot
Ground-light dun but distinct down here hugs
Munificence I eye fearfully
Forest disorder dear to Rudy

A fall night, September, black, cold
Sheen on branches from lit windows
Thin fog; before sunset not a cloud
Surveyed the lake from its marsh end
Water, many leaves shone silver
A breeze blew, whitish brilliant sky
Dark hills, dark the landscape appeared
Minutely stereoscopic
Spongy dusk was more comforting
A door slammed, cooking, greasy pots
Night has me now, by itself from
Forever, go to bed a coward
Swum supine in brightness, raised my head
Immortal shone afloat in trunks

New York dark in August, seaward
Creeping breeze, building to building
Old poems by Frank O'Hara
At 3 a.m. I sit reading
Like a blue-black surf rider, shark
Nipping at my Charvet tie, toe-tied
Heart in my mouth—or my New York
At dawn smiling I turn out the light
Inside out like a room in gritty
Gale, features moving fierce or void
Intimate, the lunch hour city
One's own heart eating undestroyed
Complicities of New York speech
Embrace me as I fall asleep

The fledgling squashed by a car-tire
On bare sand above tides hatches
Twenty years past no machines here
Then hawk, crow, fox darts and snatches
Sand-colored fluff, the parents flutter
Dive screaming; their beach safe, at me
On my dune; race, scream at each other
Half hummingbird, half eagle
White sand glares lower than dark blue
Ocean, north wind leaning tilted
Behind it, askew wild rose bush
Shivers of silver grass lift it
Day, night rotate, immensely slowed
All we survivors within float

Friends smiling step out through the door
Diminish shouts of the party
Home single undress or by pairs
Asleep lose their identity
Senseless abed, no problems, friends
Both ways, a third too, hours of work
Daily the intent absence ends
Buoyant friends daily apart lurk
Among strangers most of life laid
Like at night's trembling stasis you peer
One rooming house still bulb-lit shade
Maybe print, maybe cans of beer
Subway or street, glances smiling
Move close, turn aside, beguiling

Remote from New York, on north dunes
Remote as a child's vacant lot
Looming of oceanic noons
Gamma-ray spears of Northern Lights
Tern, rose and rabbit, their sand shared
I have the view, they reproduce
Scoot and swoop and bloom fluctuform
Wind, beast or sea, nocturnal cries
Vacationist trailers, cars, jeeps
Outboard motors, planes, helicopter
Tough as beetles, the toys of peace
Distract me more than they ought'er
By lamplight, hearing ocean roar
Drink rye, read, an interloper

OTHER POEMS

"It takes all kinds," the hackie's saw
Why he don't stop, you're the wrong kind
The cop's broadminded both sides the law
You're a questionmark in his mind
One day the public says, you fart
Another it says you're a prince
There's also the voice in your own heart
Half the time so stupid, you wince
The brightest species, we're all in it
Born with a for-nose's-sake nose
Wonder of a distant planet
Spinning, spinning, a rose is a rose
Poem or rose is a shelter
On Mother Earth till they melt her

In a hotelroom a madman
Breaks off armchair leg, brains me
Asleep; clever Paris surgeon
Extracts stomach; been killed nearly
Who hasn't, the much worse rents of love
Even of selfesteem survived
Left shamefully but glad to still live
Watch the rich hide, watch the poor hide
Death's dread; trapped I turn toward friends
Long dead when I found them, poets
Who when I'm crazed give my heart strength
By their tone of voice they do it
Some of that death-dread can be shook
Jumping across, eyes read a book

At first sight, not Pollock, Kline scared
Me, in the Cedar, ten years past
Drunk, dark-eyed, watchful, light-hearted
Everybody drunk, his wide chest
Adorable hero, mourn him
No one Franz didn't like, Elaine said
The flowered casket was loathesome
Who are we sorry for, he's dead
Between death and us his painting
Stood, we relied daily on it
To keep our hearts on the main thing
Grandeur in a happy world of shit
Walk up his stoop, 14th near 8th
The view stretches as far as death

The newspaper lies slid, tracked up
Pants lie partly deformed dropped loose
Bills, coins in an undrunk-up cup
You conked out, sheet pulled over face
You will not awake married, unmarried
Not believe, believe, you un-you
Belong, be dropped or be carried
Oh that unpredictable glue
Dear still life, sleeper, dear creature
Illuminated eye-sky-wise
Oh the recognizable feature
Which recognizes, later dies
Do I know, of course I know it
I write echoing a dead poet

In tooth and claw red, not nature
It's the evolved brain that's gory
A beast kills, forgets soon enough
We don't, old grudges, old glory
She nags, screams till he divorces
First she grabs his money, then weeps
It's normal lawyers tell clients
People normally think like creeps
A rat while dinosaurs perished
That's how modest our race was once
At present overkill's cherished
Now we're two million plus dunces
But our race'll have this epitaph
"The first to invent the word love"

Old age, lookit, it's stupid, a big fart
Messy what you are, it's preposterous
Cane slips on the kerb, helped up, he grins, part
Apologetic, watchful, vain, a mess.
And the flash phantom jumps transparent jumps
Rust flange loose, eye walked with walking sweet bees
Straw coin, sky's green pin, own heart's shrewd lumps
Its submiss trees and ancient evasive ease.
Child's shrieks left tied in the dark who falls bruised
Like a senile man's squeaks of rage at chess
Girl's gorgeous, ten feet tall, smile unconfused
I'm a fool cared for, thank you yes, age, yes, such a mess.
Cat and kittens each summer my sweetheart
Consciousness shrinks, leaves them the larger part.

[VERSION A]

Old age, lookit, it's stupid, a big fart
Messy what you are, it's preposterous
Bird cry in the dark, galumph, he plopped, part
Apologetic, watchful, vain, a mess.

And the flash phantom jumps transparent jumps
Bronze flame-out a lovely gone glitter black trees
Straw gaze, sky's green pin, deep heart's slender lumps
Dark grass-trees, and its ancient evasive ease

Unrecognizable dear friends confused
Beautiful, inviolable, gorgeous
Ten feet tall, intermittent smile like bruised
Green-dun, green blue, me too, age is a mess.

Cat and kittens each summer my sweetheart
Consciousness shrinks leaves them the larger part

[VERSION B]

THE POETRY OF EDWIN DENBY
Frank O'Hara

I have recently been rereading Mr. Denby's first book, *In Public, In Private*, a kind of "Poet in New York" with its acute and painful sensibility, its vigorous ups and downs and stubborn tone. Since its appearance in 1948, it seems an increasingly important book for the risks it takes in successfully establishing a specifically American spoken diction which has a classical firmness and clarity under his hand. He contributed then a number of our very few fine sonnets and the remarkable city-poem, "Elegy—The Streets," along with other, less perfect, but true, vital poems.

Mediterranean Cities is a handsome publication, printed in Italy and adorned with photographs by Rudolph Burckhardt, the gifted artist and film-maker. The new poems are sonnets on places and, as in Proust, the artist's feelings become the sensibility of the places; *Mediterranean Cities* follows a Proustian progression of sensation, reflection, awareness, spontaneous memory and apotheosis, a progression which proceeds from the signal absorption in locale ("place names") and its accidental characteristics to the emergence of the poet's being from his feelings in "the place." The poet himself eventually is the place.

While the interior of the sequence, the book as a whole, is related to Proust's method in my mind, another reference suggests itself. Unlike the many poems-about-Europe-by-Americans we have had recently, the "Fulbright poems" as someone recently described them, Mr. Denby's sonnets are in the great tradition of the Romantics, and particularly Shelley. With similar delicacy and opacity, and with a great deal more economy, he fixes the shifting moods, the sympathetic grasp of meaning in what the vulgar see only as picturesque, the pervading melancholy which overcomes the poet when he unites with the inanimate; this all reminds one of the English Romantic poets on the Continent, and is reinforced by a cultural maturity like that of the Romantics (whatever one may think of their emotional status) which has seldom been achieved by an American poet in specific relation to the European past and his own present. But, being the work of a modern poet, Mr. Denby's sonnets do not rise up to end in a burst of passionate identification, they light up from within with a kind of Mallarméan lucidity. They are obscure poems, eminently worth understanding, and I find these references helpful, though they may seem to leap about. One of Mallarmé's favorite poems, after all, was by Shelley.

Unless I am very much mistaken, the sequence of the poems (it is not called a sonnet sequence) is very important, and concerns itself with evaluations of art and life, historical and personal, in a serious lyrical manner which, being itself art, is also graceful. Sometimes the poet is isolated before the subject, the self evaluating the subject in traditional fashion:

> Who watched Antinous in the yellow water
> Here where swollen plains gully, Roman and brown
> Built for fun, before a flat horizon scattered
> Fancies, such advanced ones, that lie overthrown;
> Urbanely they still leer, his voided surprises
> Curved reflections, double half-lights, coigns of rest
> Embarrassing as a rich man without admirers
> Peculiar like a middle-aged man undressed;
> Over the view's silent groundswell floats a field
> Enskied by one eerie undeviating wall
> Far to a door; pointing up his quietude
> Watchful Hadrian exudes a sour smell;
> The ratty smell of spite, his wit, his laughter
> Who watched Antinous smile in yellow water

This, for the reader, is a sort of landscape-with-poet, and presently we find the picture changing: it is the poet-in-landscape; not the physical prospect, but the past of the place has begun to absorb him.

> Are you Russians the boys said seeing us strange
> Easy in grace by a poster with bicycles
> Soft voices in a Baroque and Byzantine slum
> Lemon pickers by swelling seas rainbow-fickle;
> On the height drizzle, and among thyme and mint
> A small shepherd, a large canvas umbrella
> Leaps away down the crumbled ruins, timid
> Where once they fought in moonlight, and Athens fell

And this becomes not merely being in a foreign place, a stranger to its myriad times, but also to one's own history:

> Harbor, lost is the Greece when I was ten that
> Seduced me, god-like it shone; in a dark town, trembling
> Like a runaway boy on his first homeless night
> Ahead I rush in the fearful sweep of longing
> A dead longing that all day blurred here the lone
> Clear shapes which light was defining for a grown man

In a climactic moment the poet finds in himself the living sentence of a culture which may be dying, but is slow to die, is living for his sake, the ambiguous nature of temporality made clear by the timeless exertion of consciousness:

> She lifts from men dead into my passing life
> A beauty of doubt that is homeless and not brief

It seems to me that Mr. Denby in these sonnets has created something modern and intrinsic, sensitive and strong. Incidentally he seems to have lifted William Carlos Williams' famous moratorium on the sonnet . . . But to close:

> Now in New York Jacob wants to have my cat
> He goes to school, he behaves aggressively
> He is three and a half, age makes us do that
> And fifty years hence will he love Rome in place of me?
> For with regret I leave the lovely world men made
> Despite their bad character, their art is mild

Mr. Denby's own art has the classical gift for giving, in the present tense.

1957

ON EDWIN DENBY
Lincoln Kirstein

Edwin Denby is well known as a dance critic. By the time he was sixty, the two volumes of his collected notices from the Forties and Fifties were taken as basic theatrical history.[1] Although his particular attention referred to performances no longer visible, moral and aesthetic judgment illuminated current parallels. His analyses were superbly constructed, usually constructive, and warmly glowing with an absolute love of the art. They also had a scalpel's delicate, sanitary edge when detecting a spot as false. His prose was didactic, schooling those in the audience willing to be more than lightly amused. He taught three generations to see more than they had first suspected, and inspired more than one young English literature major to think with care about writing on dancing.

Edwin was a great dance critic primarily because he was a fine poet. His poems, while collected and well presented in 1975,[2] through the enthusiasm of close friends, are available today for readers who prize good verse as much as good dancing. He is not anthologized. Modern literature courses don't take much account of him, nor is he treated as an important lyricist by many beyond a band of admirers, too often discounted as a coterie. But some poets, now far more fully published, appreciate such poetry; this was the only fame he liked. He accepted the nomination of journalist, but craft and insight lifted him to the level of professional artist. In his elegy, "Snoring in New York," he presents himself:

> Summer New York, friends tonight at cottages
> I lie motionless, a single retired man
> White-haired, ferrety, feminine, religious
> I look like a priest, a detective, a con
> Nervously I step among the city crowd
> My private life of no interest and allowed
>
> Brutality or invisibility
> We have for one another and to ourselves
> Gossamer-like lifts the transparent city
> Its levitating and ephemeral shelves
> So shining, so bridged, so demolished a woof
> Towers and holes we sit in that gales put to proof

It is hardly by chance that the most thorough writers concerned with dance were prime poets—Théophile Gautier, Stéphane Mallarmé, Paul

[1] *Looking at the Dance* and *Dancers, Buildings and People in the Streets.*
[2] *Collected Poems.*

Valéry. Other verse makers who observed dancing with some attention, but are rarely read for it, are Federico García Lorca and Hart Crane. It is to these master choreographers of words that Denby is most akin.

When his verse is read with the care it deserves and commands, he may be recognized as the clearest lyric voice of Manhattan since Crane's epopoeia of the Brooklyn Bridge. He shares Crane's quirkiness in implosive short circuits of dense, awkwardly precise rhetoric, odd broken rhymes, reckless rhythm, sharpness of physical imagery and incandescent metaphor. There is a sense of place, of American loneliness similar to that in some of Edward Hopper's paintings. Crane was a hysteric, his hysteria increasing tragically from self-inflamed euphoria. Compulsive self-indulgence did him in early on. Denby was a survivor, who put an end to himself only when old, when he could no longer manage his body. This he accomplished, with much good work behind him, large in instruction and influence. He endured unspoken pain and took a stoic exit, disdaining to burden further his friends or himself. This is a matter more for celebration than for sadness.

His poetry concerns cities in history, past and present, European and American, detailed with domestic intimacy, an experienced tourist's familiarity. Rudy Burckhardt, his lifelong friend and illuminator, provided a visual gloss on specific sites. Controlled accident in snapshots is always present in Edwin's imagery. He had a "photographic" eye and a powerful visual memory. The atmosphere, societies, and qualities of many cities, Mediterranean and American, form an album of superpostcards, more real than any nostalgic material souvenir.

> I stroll on Madison in expensive clothes, sour.
> Ostrich-legg'd or sweet-chested, the loping clerks
> Slide me a glance nude as oh in a tiled shower
> And lope on dead-pan, large male and female jerks.
>
> Later from the open meadow in the Park
> I watch a bulging pea-soup storm lie midtown;
> Here the high air is clear, there buildings are murked,
> Manhattan absorbs the cloud like a sage-brush plain.
>
> In the grass sleepers sprawl without attraction:
> Some large men who turned sideways, old ones on papers,
> A soldier, face handkerchiefed, an erection
> In his pants—only men, the women don't nap here.
>
> Can these wide spaces suit a particular man?
> They can suit whomever man's intestines can.

García Lorca, in exile at Columbia University, was miserable in Manhattan. Nevertheless, out of misery, he composed his memorable portrait of Walt Whitman, another psalmist of cities. Whitman's voice resounds in García Lorca, Crane, and Denby, not only for their "love of comrades" and "sleepers," but in their substantial miniatures of cityscapes, their crowds, corner bars, shops which frame fierce and tender lives. There is a short-breathed sonnet by Denby, "On the Home Front—1942," encapsulating a moment in our national story, as every famous wartime photograph does, and its final couplet makes a generalization which is also the portrait of its poet:

> The small survivor has a difficult task
> Answering the questions great historians ask.

Edwin's presence was that of a dancer. Forty years ago he looked like a boy retired from ballet. His trimness and courtesy never left him. Quiet elegance solidified in a firm aura while his handsome head turned gray to white. His presence at performances of the New York City Ballet was steady reassurance to the company; while his fair opinion was always hoped for, his silent authority made any casual gossip superfluous.

His essay on Stravinsky and Balanchine's *Agon* (1957) is the most telling and comprehensive technical appreciation of a dance work that has been written. To be able to make visible in words what was, and is, difficult to grasp by eyes alone, treating steps lacking any narrative pretext, is in itself a tour de force, more exhausting than any thirty-two *fouettés en tournant*. Denby's degree of penetration touching the irreducible skeleton of a masterpiece was equivalent in quality to the matters in question.

Many attached to classic academic ballet read his particulars of performance as sturdy correctives. He loved every tribe of dancer, traditional, ethnic, experimental, popular. He had no preconceived prejudice and was not the keeper of any personal, possessive flame. He tended to lean eagerly toward pioneers, not only giving newcomers benefit of doubt for their daring, but because he delighted in and was amused by any effort to budge human bodies in alternatives to habit.

Balanchine talked little and thought less about journalism covering dance events. Actually, he read everything he laid his hands on relative to his own company, while steadfastly denying this. However, it amounted to the same thing, since he was so secure in his own opinion that he disqualified columns he found irrelevant as nonexistent. After all, dance critics, like cobblers, had to earn their living. But after reading Edwin's extraordinary essay on *Agon* he sent it to Stravinsky.

When Balanchine read Denby's criticism of *Concerto Barocco*, he told Richard Buckle, "If you must write, try writing like that." Buckle replied sadly: *"But I'm not a dancer. . . ."* Edwin was trained as a dancer: he knew in his own bone, mind and muscle how dancers feel about how they step. Gautier, Mallarmé, Valéry, were not dancers, but their gifts as lyric poets fulfilled the discrepancy. Edwin was both dancer and poet. His prose is textbook information, chapter *and* verse.

Some of us believe in the beauty and scope of his songs (written for Aaron Copland's operas), his sonnets, his elegiac praise of towns, his strong sense of the inhalation and exhalation of peoples, day and night, in their mass, in their individuality. Here is scent and sense not to be found in any other "modern" American versifier. This, a second stanza from "Groups and Series":

> In enterprise, in sleep, how well men wear
> the shifting illuminations of the air:
> watching a sleeper we will come to trust
> the body anchored in its breathing's thrust;
> loosened in sleep, his weight lies there as such,
> rounded in all this moonlight, cool to touch.
> Beside you, broken by the lamp's short beams,
> he shows you shadows black as parts of dreams.

1983

WORKS BY EDWIN DENBY

POETRY

In Public, In Private, two editions. Prairie City, Illinois: The Press of James A. Decker, 1948.
Mediterranean Cities. New York: Wittenborn, 1956.
"C" Magazine. Vol. 1, No. 4, Special Denby Issue. New York: September 1963.
Snoring in New York. New York: Angel Hair/Adventures in Poetry, 1974.
Collected Poems. New York: Full Court Press, 1975.
The Complete Poems. New York: Random House, 1986.

FICTION

Mrs. W's Last Sandwich. Original title: *Scream in a Cave*. New York: Horizon, 1972.
Scream in a Cave. New York: Curtis Books, 1973.

CRITICISM

Ballet. New York: J. J. Augustin, 1945.
Looking at the Dance. New York: Pellegrini and Cudahy, 1949; New York: Horizon, 1968; New York: Curtis Books, 1973; New York: Popular Library, 1978.
Dancers, Buildings and People in the Streets. New York: Horizon, 1965; New York: Curtis Books, 1973; New York: Popular Library, 1979.
Dance Writings. New York: Knopf, 1986.

LIBRETTOS

The Second Hurricane. New York: Boosey and Hawkes, 1957.
Miltie Is a Hackie. Calais, Vermont: Z Press, 1973.
The Sonntag Gang. In *Mag City* 14, Special Denby Issue. New York: 1983.

ADAPTATIONS

Die Neue Galathea. Mainz, Germany: B. Schott's Sons, 1929.
Horse Eats Hat, with Orson Welles (unpublished).
The Criminals, with Rita Matthias (unpublished).

EDITED

Aerial. New York: Eyelight Press, 1981.

OTHER

Two Conversations with Edwin Denby. New York: Byrd Hoffman Foundation, 1974.

INDEX OF TITLES AND FIRST LINES

191

ABOUT THE AUTHOR

EDWIN DENBY was born in Tientsin, China, in 1903, and was raised in China, Austria, and the United States. He attended Harvard and later studied dance in Vienna, after which he and a friend formed a dance company that performed in Germany from 1928 to 1933. After 1935, he lived mainly in New York. He died in Searsmont, Maine, in 1983.

Besides his poetry and librettos, Denby also wrote renowned dance criticism. His collection of writings on the dance will be published later this year by Alfred A. Knopf.